The Suffrage

Mrs. L. O. Kleber

Alpha Editions

This edition published in 2024

ISBN : 9789364736619

Design and Setting By
Alpha Editions
www.alphaedis.com
Email - info@alphaedis.com

As per information held with us this book is in Public Domain.
This book is a reproduction of an important historical work. Alpha Editions uses the best technology to reproduce historical work in the same manner it was first published to preserve its original nature. Any marks or number seen are left intentionally to preserve its true form.

CONTENTS

Introduction .... - 1 -

SOUPS .... - 4 -

War Not Only Kills Bodies But Ideals .... - 10 -

MEATS, POULTRY, ETC. .... - 15 -

VEGETABLES .... - 31 -

SAVORIES .... - 41 -

BREAD, ROLLS, ETC. .... - 43 -

CAKES, COOKIES, TARTS, ETC. .... - 54 -

PASTRIES, PIES, ETC. .... - 70 -

PUDDINGS .... - 73 -

SANDWICH RECIPES .... - 80 -

SALADS AND SALAD DRESSINGS .... - 82 -

COLORED SALADS .... - 85 -

MEAT and FISH SAUCES .... - 90 -

EGGS, ETC. .... - 92 -

CREAMS, CUSTARDS, ETC. .... - 95 -

PRESERVES, PICKLES, ETC. .... - 100 -

CANDIES, ETC. .... - 106 -

ALBUMINOUS BEVERAGES .... - 110 -

STARCHY BEVERAGES .... - 117 -

THE COOK SAYS .... - 121 -

Economical Soap .... - 124 -

INTRODUCTION

There are cook books and cook books, and their generation is not ended; a generation that began in the Garden of Eden, presumably, for if Mother Eve was not vastly different from her daughters she knew how to cook some things better than her neighbors, and they wanted to know how she made them and she wanted to tell them.

Indeed, it has been stated that the very first book printed, a small affair, consisted mainly of recipes for "messes" of food, and for remedies for diseases common in growing families.

Whether the very first book printed was a cook book or not, it is quite true that among the very oldest books extant are those telling how to prepare food, clothing and medicine. Some of these make mighty interesting reading, particularly the portions relating to cures for all sorts of ills, likewise of love when it seemed an ill, and of ill luck.

And who wouldn't cheerfully pay money, even in this enlightened day, for a book containing recipes for just these same things? For in spite of our higher civilization, broader education, and vastly extended knowledge, we still believe in lucky days, lucky stones, and lucky omens.

These formed no inconsiderable part of the old time cook book, and no doubt would constitute a very attractive feature of a modern culinary guide. However, hardly anyone would confess to having bought it on that account.

In these later times professors of the culinary art tell us the cooking has been reduced to a science, and that there is no more guess work about it. They have given high sounding names to the food elements, figured out perfectly balanced rations, and adjusted foods to all conditions of health, or ill health. And yet the world is eating practically the same old things, and in the same old way, the difference being confined mainly to the sauces added to please the taste.

Now that women are coming into their own, and being sincerely interested in the welfare of the race, it is entirely proper that they should prescribe the food, balance the ration, and tell how it should be prepared and served.

Seeing that a large majority of the sickness that plagues the land is due to improper feeding, and can be prevented by teaching the simple art of cooking, of serving and of eating, the wonder is that more attention has not been given to instruction in the simpler phases of the culinary art.

It is far from being certain that famous chefs have contributed greatly to the health and long life of those able to pay the fine salaries they demand. Nor are these sent to minister to the sick, nor to the working people, nor to the poor. It would seem that even since before the time of Lucullus their business has been mainly to invent and concoct dishes that would appeal to perverted tastes and abnormal appetites.

The simple life promises most in this earthly stage of our existence, for as we eat so we live, and as we live so we die, and after death the judgment on our lives. Thus it is that our spiritual lives are more or less directly influenced by our feeding habits.

Eating and drinking are so essential to our living and to our usefulness, and so directly involved with our future state, that these must be classed with our sacred duties. Hence the necessity for so educating the children that they will know how to live, and how to develop into hale, hearty and wholesome men and women, thus insuring the best possible social and political conditions for the people of this country.

"The surest way into the affections of a man is through his stomach, also to his pocket," is an ancient joke, and yet not all a joke, there being several grains of truth in it, enough at least to warrant some thoughtful attention.

Women being the homekeepers, and the natural guardians of the children, it is important that they be made familiar with the culinary art so they may be entirely competent to lead coming generations in the paths of health and happiness.

So say the members of Equal Franchise Associations throughout the length and breadth of our land, and beyond the border as far as true civilization extends.

Hence this book which represents an honest effort to benefit the people, old and young, native and foreign. It is not a speculative venture but a dependable guide to a most desirable social, moral and physical state of being.

Disguise it as we may the fact remains that the feeding of a people is of first importance, seeing the feeding is the great essential to success, either social or commercial. The farmer and stock raiser gives special attention to feeding, usually more to the feeding of his animals than of his children, or of himself. And yet he wonders why his domestic affairs do not thrive and prosper as does his farming and stock raising.

Physical trainers are most particular about what the members of their classes eat and drink. One mess of strawberry short cake and cream will unfit a boy for a field contest for a whole week, while a full meal of dainties may completely upset a man or woman for a day or two.

The cook book of the past was filled mainly with recipes for dainties rather than sane and wholesome dishes; the aim being to please the taste for the moment rather than to feed the body and the brain.

Now that we are entering upon an age of sane living it is important that the home makers should be impressed with the fact that good health precedes all that is worth while in life, and that it starts in the kitchen; that the dining room is a greater social factor than the drawing room.

In the broader view of the social world that is dawning upon us the cook book that tells us how to live right and well will largely supplant Shakespeare, Browning, and the lurid literature of the day.

ERASMUS WILSON
(The Quiet Observer)

The tocsin of the soul—the dinner bell.

—Byron.

As it is a serious matter *what* is put into the human stomach, I feel it incumbent to say that my readers may safely eat everything set down in this book.

Most recipes have been practically tested by me, and those of which I have not eaten coming with such unquestionable authority, there need be no hesitancy in serving them alike to best friend as well as worst enemy—for I believe in the one case it will strengthen friendship, and in the other case it will weaken enmity.

It being a human Cook Book there will likely be some errors, but as correcting errors is the chief duty and occupation of Suffrage Women, I shall accept gratefully whatever criticisms these good women may have to offer.

I thank all for the courtesy shown me and hope our united efforts will prove helpful to the Great Cause.

I ask pardon for any omission of contributors and their recipes.

Mrs. L. O. Kleber.

SOUPS

Asparagus Soup

4 bunches asparagus
1 small onion
1 pint milk
½ pint cream
1½ tablespoon sugar
1 large tablespoon butter
1½ tablespoon flour
pepper to season

Wash and clean asparagus, put in saucepan with just enough water to cover, boil until little points are soft.

Cut these off and lay aside. Fry onion in the butter and put in saucepan with the asparagus. Cook until very soft mashing occasionally so as to extract all juice from the asparagus.

When thoroughly cooked put through sieve. Now add salt, sugar and flour blended.

Stir constantly and add milk and cream, and serve at once. (Do not place again on stove as it might curdle. Croutons may be served with this).

Spinach Soup

½ peck spinach
2 tablespoons butter
1½ tablespoon sugar
1½ teaspoons salt
1 small onion
1 pint rich milk
2 tablespoons flour
½ cup water

Put spinach in double boiler with the butter and water. Let simmer slowly until all the juice has been extracted from the spinach.

Fry the onion and add. Now thicken with the flour blended with the water and strain. Add the milk very hot. Do not place on the fire after the milk has been added.

Half cream instead of milk greatly improves flavor.

Crab Gumbo

3 doz. medium Okra
1 doz. Crabs cleaned
2 onions fried

Add the Crabs, then small can tomatoes. Thyme, parsley, bay leaf.

Tomato Soup

1 large can tomatoes or equivalent of fresh tomatoes.
1 small onion
1 tablespoon salt
dash paprika
2½ tablespoons sugar
1 tablespoon butter
2½ tablespoons flour
2 cups hot milk
1 pint water

Put tomatoes with 1 pt. water to boil, boil for at least half hour. Fry onion in butter and add to soup with sugar and salt. When thoroughly cooked thicken with the flour blended with a little water. Now strain. Have the milk very hot, not boiling. Stir constantly while adding milk to soup and serve at once.

Do not place on the stove after the milk is in the soup. 1 cup of cream instead of 2 cups of milk greatly improves the soup.

Vegetable Soup

2½ lbs. of beef (with soup bone)
3 quarts of water
1 tablespoon sugar
salt to suit taste
a few pepper corns
1 cup of each, of the following vegetables
diced small
carrots
Potatoes
Celery
2 tablespoons onion cut very fine
½ head cabbage cut very fine
½ can corn (or its equivalent in fresh)
½ can peas (or its equivalent fresh)
2 tablespoons minced parsley
¼ cup turnip and parsnip if at hand (not necessary)

½ can tomatoes (or equivalent fresh)

Put meat in large kettle and boil for an hour; now add all the other ingredients and cook until soft. Ready then to serve.

This soup can be made as a cream soup without meat and is delicious. In this case you take a good sized piece of butter and fry all the vegetables slightly, excepting the potatoes. Now cover all, adding potatoes with boiling water and cook until tender.

When done season and add hot milk and 1 cup cream. This is very fine.

In making this soup without meat omit the tomatoes and use string beans instead.

Tell me what you eat, and I'll tell you what you are.

Brillat Savarin.

Chestnut Soup

1 qt. chestnuts (Spanish preferred)
1 pint chicken stock
2 tablespoons flour
1 teaspoon sugar
salt and paprika to taste

Cover chestnuts with boiling water slightly salted. Cook until quite soft and rub through coarse sieve, add stock, and seasoning; then thicken with flour blended with water.

Let simmer five minutes and serve at once.

In case stock is not available milk can be used with a little butter added.

Peanut Butter Broth

1 pt. fresh sweet milk
1 pt. water
1½ tablespoons peanut butter
1 tablespoon catsup
Salt, pepper or other season to taste.

Pour liquid with peanut butter into double boiler; dissolve butter so there are no hard lumps. Do not let milk boil but place on moderately hot fire.

Just before serving add the catsup and seasoning.

Soup for Invalids

Cut into small pieces one pound of beef or mutton or a part of both. Boil it gently in two quarts of water. Take off the scum and when reduced to a pint, strain it and season with a little salt. Give one teacupful at a time.

Peanut Soup

Peanut soup for supper on a cold night serves the double duty of stimulating the gastric juices to quicken action by its warmth and furnishing protein to the body to repair its waste. Pound to a paste a cupful of nuts from which the skin has been removed, add it to a pint of milk and scald; melt a tablespoon of butter and mix it with a like quantity of flour and add slowly to the milk and peanuts; cook until it thickens and season to taste.

Chestnuts, too, make a splendid soup. Boil one quart of peeled and blanched chestnuts in three pints of salt water until quite soft; pass through sieve and add two tablespoons of sweet cream, and season to taste. If too thick, add water.

Mock Oyster Soup

The oyster plant is used for this delicious dish—by many it is known as salsify. Scrape the vegetable and cut into small pieces with a silver knife (a steel knife would darken the oyster plant). Cook in just enough water to keep from burning, and when tender press through a colander and return to the water in which it was cooked. Add three cups of hot milk which has been thickened with a little butter and flour and rubbed together and seasoned with salt and white pepper. A little chopped parsley may be added before serving. ½ cup cream instead of all milk greatly improves taste.

French Oyster Soup

1 quart oysters
1 quart milk
1 slice onion
2 blades mace
$1/3$ cup flour
$1/3$ cup butter
2 egg yolks
salt and pepper

Clean oysters by pouring over ¾ cup cold water. Drain, reserve liquor, add oysters, slightly chopped, heat slowly to boiling point and let simmer 20 minutes; strain.

Scald milk with onion and mace. Make white sauce and add oyster liquor. Just before serving add egg yolks, slightly beaten.

Split Pea Soup (Green or Yellow)

1½ pints split peas (green or yellow)
2¼ quarts water
2 small onions
1 carrot
1 parsnip (if at hand)
1 cup milk
½ cup cream
1 teaspoon salt (more if liked)
Pepper and paprika to taste
1½ teaspoons sugar

Soak 1½ pints of split peas over night; next day add 2¼ quarts water and the vegetables, cut fine; also the sugar, salt and pepper and cook slowly three hours; now mash through sieve. If it boils down too much add a little water. After putting through sieve place on stove and add hot milk and cream. If it is not thin enough to suit add more milk.

Stock may be used if same is available.

Black Bean Soup

One pint of black beans soaked over night in 3 quarts of water.

In the morning pour off the water and add fresh 3 quarts. Boil slowly 4 hours. When done there should be 1 quart. Add a quart of beef stock, 4 whole cloves, 4 whole allspice, 1 stalk of celery, 1 good sized onion, 1 small carrot, 1 small turnip, all cut fine and fried in a little butter.

Add 1 tablespoon flour, season with salt and pepper and rub through a fine sieve.

Serve with slices of lemon and egg balls.

Carrot Soup

One quart of thinly sliced carrots, one head of celery, three or four quarts of water, boil for two and one-half hours; add one-half cupful of rice and boil for an hour longer; season with salt and pepper and a small cupful of cream.

Veal Soup

Knuckle of veal 2½ pounds
2 raw eggs
3 quarts water
2 tomatoes cut fine
½ onion
salt and pepper to season

a little flour
½ cup vermicelli or alphabet macaroni
2 eggs, beaten very light
1½ tablespoons parmesan cheese

Put veal in stewing pan and allow it to cook until thoroughly done. Now chop meat and add cheese, flour, salt and pepper if needed and form into little balls about the size of a marble. While preparing these, drop in macaroni and cook until tender. Now add the meat balls.

If too thick use a little water. Beat the eggs lightly and add while boiling.

WAR NOT ONLY KILLS BODIES BUT IDEALS

MRS. HENRY VILLARD,
President of Women's Peace Conference.

Must the pride with which women point to the life saving character of the work of the numberless charitable agencies throughout the country—with a resultant lowering of the death rate in our great cities—be offset by the slaughter of our best beloved ones on the field of battle or their death by disease in camps?

No longer ought we to be called upon to be particeps criminis with men to the extent of being compelled to pay taxes which are largely used for the support of the army and navy.

Moreover, a recourse to war as a means of righting wrongs is full of peril to the whole human race. Not only are bodies killed, but the ideals which alone make life worth living are for the time being lost to sight. In place of those finer attributes of our nature—compassion, gentleness, forgiveness—are substituted hatred, revenge and cruelty.

He was a bold man that first ate an oyster.—Swift.

Virginia Fried Oysters

Make a batter of four tablespoons of sifted flour, one tablespoon of olive oil or melted butter, two well-beaten whites of eggs, one-half teaspoon of salt, and warm water enough to make a batter that will drop easily. Sprinkle the oysters lightly with salt and white pepper or paprika. Dip in the batter and fry to a golden brown.

Drain, and serve on a hot platter, with slices of lemon around them.

Creamed Lobster

2 tablespoons butter
1½ pints milk
2 tablespoons flour
season to taste

When cooked beat in the yolk of an egg.

Pick to pieces 1 can of lobster, juice of 1 onion, juice of 1 lemon, stalk of celery chopped fine, paprika, sweet peppers, cut fine. Mix all together and serve in ramekins. Serve very hot. Serves 12 people.

Salmon Croquettes

Fresh salmon or 1 can of salmon
2 eggs
½ cup butter
1 cup fine bread crumbs
1 teaspoon baking powder
½ cup of cream
1 pinch of paprika
salt to season

Mix well and form into croquettes. Roll in egg and cracker crumbs and fry in deep fat.

Partial suffrage has taught the women of Illinois the value of political power and direct influence. Already the effect of the ballot has been shown in philanthropic, civic and social work in which women are engaged and the women of this state realizing that partial suffrage means so much to them, wish to express their deepest interest in the outcome of the campaign for full suffrage which eastern women are waging this year.

So we say to the women in the four campaign states this year: "You are working not only toward your own enfranchisement but toward the enfranchisement of the women in all the non-suffrage states in the union. Your victory means victory in other states. You are our leaders at this crucial time and thousands of women are looking to you. You have their deepest and heartiest co-operation in your campaign work for much depends upon what you do in working for that victory which we hope will come to the women of Pennsylvania, New York, New Jersey and Massachusetts in this year of 1915."

JANE ADDAMS.

Broiled Salt Mackerel

Wash and scrape the fish. Soak all night, changing the water at bed time for tepid and again early in the morning for almost scalding hot. Keep this hot for an hour by setting the vessel containing the soaking fish on the side of the range. Wash next in cold water with a stiff brush or rough cloth, wipe perfectly dry, rub all over again with salad oil and vinegar or lemon juice and let it lie in this marmalade for a quarter of an hour before broiling. Place on a hot dish with a mixture of butter, lemon juice and minced parsley.

Shrimp Wriggle

1 pint fresh shrimps

1 heaping cup hot boiled rice

1 medium size green pepper

1 tablespoonful Worcestershire sauce

2 tablespoons tomato catsup

1 scant pint cream with heaping teaspoon flour

butter size of egg

paprika and salt to taste.

Dissolve flour in cream, add shrimps, rice, pepper (chopped), pour in cream, add butter, add condiments, add just before serving 1 wineglass sherry or Madeira.

HELEN RING ROBINSON.

Chop Suey

Chop Suey is made of chopped meat and the gizzards of ducks or chickens, 1 cup of chopped celery and ½ cup of shredded almonds.

Mix with the following sauce: 1 tablespoon butter and 1 teaspoon arrow root stirred into 1 cupful broth. Add 1 teaspoon worcestershire sauce and simmer all for twenty minutes.

Veal Kidney Stew

1 veal kidney

1 small onion

1 tablespoon butter

2 tomatoes cut fine

1 small can mushrooms

½ tablespoon parsley

4 tablespoons raw potatoes cut in small pieces

Seasoning to taste

Wash, clean and cut fine a veal kidney. Fry onion in butter until light brown, add kidney, tomatoes, mushrooms, parsley, potatoes, seasoning and water, and cook until tender.

MEATS, POULTRY, ETC.

Baked Ham

(a la Miller)

1 ten or twelve pound ham

1½ lb. brown sugar

1 pint sherry wine (cooking sherry)

1 cup vinegar (not too strong)

1 cup molasses

cloves (whole)

Scrub and cleanse ham; soak in cold water over night; in morning place in a large kettle and cover with cold water; bring slowly to the boiling point and gradually add the molasses, allowing 18 minutes for each pound. When ham is done remove from stove and allow it to become cold in the water in which it was cooked.

Now remove the ham from water; skin and stick cloves (about 1½ dozen) over the ham. Rub brown sugar into the ham; put in roasting pan and pour over sherry and vinegar. Baste continually and allow it to warm through and brown nicely. This should take about ½ hour. Serve with a garnish of glazed sweet potatoes. Caramel from ham is served in a gravy tureen. Remove all greases from same.

This is a dish fit for the greatest epicure.

Man is a carnivorous production and must have meals, at least one meal a day. He cannot live like wood cocks, upon suction. But like the shark and tiger, must have prey. Although his anatomical construction, bears vegetables, in a grumbling way. Your laboring people think beyond all question. Beef, veal and mutton, better for digestion.   Byron.

Daube

    4 lb. rump (Larded with bacon)

    2 large onions

    2 tablespoons flour

    1 small can tomatoes

    1 cup water

    1 clove garlic

    2 sprigs thyme—1 bay leaf

    ¼ sweet pepper

    several carrots

    parsley

First fry meat, then remove to platter. Start gravy by first frying the onions a nice brown; then add flour and brown; drain the tomatoes and fry; add rest of ingredients; put meat into this and let it cook slowly for five to six hours.

U. S. DEPARTMENT OF LABOR
CHILDREN'S BUREAU
WASHINGTON

November 24, 1914.

Editress Suffrage Cook Book:

Your letter of November 21st is received.

Will the following be of any use for the Suffrage Cook Book?

Is it not strange how custom can stale our sense of the importance of everyday occurrences, of the ability required for the performance of homely, everyday services? Think of the power of organization required to prepare a meal and place it upon the table on time! No wonder a mere man said, "I can't cook because of the awful simultaneousness of everything."

Yours faithfully,
JULIA C. LATHROP.

Glen Ellen,
Sonoma Co., California.
YACHT ROAMER
November 5, 1914.

Editress Suffrage Cook Book:

Forgive the long delay in replying to your letter. You see, I am out on a long cruise on the Bay of San Francisco, and up the rivers of California, and receive my mail only semi-occasionally. Yours has now come to hand, and I have consulted with Mrs. London, and we have worked out the following recipes, which are especial "tried" favorites of mine:

Roast Duck

The only way in the world to serve a canvas-back or a mallard, or a sprig, or even the toothsome teal, is as follows: The plucked bird should be stuffed with a tight handful of plain raw celery and, in a piping oven, roasted variously 8, 9, 10, or even 11 minutes, according to size of bird and heat of oven. The blood-rare breast is carved with the leg and the carcass then thoroughly squeezed in a press. The resultant liquid is seasoned with salt, pepper, lemon and paprika, and poured hot over the meat. This method of roasting insures the maximum tenderness and flavor in the bird. The longer the wild duck is roasted, the dryer and tougher it becomes.

Hoping that you may find the foregoing useful for your collection, and with best wishes for the success of your book.

Sincerely yours,
JACK LONDON.

Veal Loaf

3 pounds Veal

¼ lb. Salt Pork

1 teaspoon salt

¼ teaspoon pepper.

Of the following mixture

¼ teaspoon sage, thyme, and sweet marjoram

2 eggs

1 cup stock. If not procurable use ½ cup water and ½ cup milk

¾ cup bread crumbs

Have meat ground fine as possible. Then mix thoroughly with the herbs, 1 egg, pepper and salt, ½ cup stock and ½ cup crumbs.

Form a loaf and brush top and sides with the second egg. Now, scatter the remaining ¼ cup of crumbs over the moistened loaf.

Place in a baking pan with the ½ cup of stock and bake in a moderate oven three hours, basting very frequently, and adding water in case stock is consumed.

Ducks

Take two young ducks, wash and dry out thoroughly; rub outside with salt and pepper—lay in roasting pan, breast down. Cut in half one good sized onion and an apple cut in half (not peeled). Lay around the ducks and put in about one and one-half pints hot water. Cover with lid of roasting pan and cook in a medium hot oven.

In an hour turn ducks on back and add a teaspoon of tart jelly. Leave lid off and baste frequently.

In another hour the ducks are ready to serve. Pour off fat in pan. Make thickening for gravy (not removing the onion or apple).

For the filling, take stale loaf of bread, cut off crust and rub the bread into crumbs, dissolve a little butter (about one tablespoon), add that to the crumbs. Salt and pepper to taste and as much parsley as is desired. Mix and stuff the ducks.

From the standpoint of Science, Health, Beauty and Usefulness, the Art of Cooking leads all the other arts,—for does not the preservation of the race depend upon it?   L. P. K.

Blanquette of Veal

2 cups cold roast veal

3 teaspoons cream

2 teaspoons flour

yolks of 2 eggs

20 or 30 small onions, the kind used for pickling.

Saute the veal a moment in butter or lard without browning. Sprinkle with flour and add water making a white sauce. Add any gravy you may have left over, or 2 or 3 bouillon cubes and the onions and let cook ¾ of an hour on slow fire. Just before serving add yolks of eggs mixed with cream.

Cook for a moment, sprinkle with finely chopped parsley and serve.

Spitine

Cut from raw roast beef very thin slices. Spread with a dressing made of grated bread crumbs, a beaten egg and seasoned to taste. Roll up and put all on a long skewer and brown in a little hot butter.

Risotti a la Milanaise

2 lbs. rice

1 chicken

1 can mushrooms

1 lump butter

Parmesan cheese

Cut up chicken and cook in water as for stewing, seasoning to taste. When almost done add mushrooms and cook a little longer. Now put a large lump of butter in a pan and after washing the rice in several waters, dry on a clean napkin, and add to butter, stirring constantly. Do not allow it to darken. Cook about ten minutes and remove from fire. Take baking dish and put the rice in bottom. Now sprinkle generously with parmesan cheese. Cut chicken up and remove all bones, pour over rice and cook until dry, adding gravy from time to time.

This can be eaten hot or cold.

Der Mensch ist was er iszt.   German.

Liver Dumplings (Leber Kloese)

1 calf's liver

1/8 lb. Suet

1 small onion

¼ loaf bread

3 eggs

2 tablespoons bread crumbs

Salt, pepper and Sweet marjorie to taste.

Soak liver in cold water for one hour, then skin and scrape it and run it through meat chopper twice; the second time adding the suet. Brown finely cut onion in two tablespoons of lard; add salt, pepper and sweet marjorie to taste.

Soak ¼ loaf bread in cold water, squeeze out the water and mix the bread with the liver, then add three well beaten eggs and enough flour to stiffen. Drop one dumpling with a spoon into one gallon of water (slightly salted), should it cook away, then add more flour before cooking the remainder of the mixture.

Boil thirty minutes, and longer if necessary. When properly cooked the middle of the dumpling will be white.

Before serving, brown bread crumbs in butter and sprinkle over the dumplings.

A Baked Ham

Should be Kentucky cured and at least two years old. Soak in water over night.

Put on stove in cold water. Let it simmer one hour for each pound. Allow it to stand in that water over night.

Remove skin, cover with brown sugar and biscuit or cracker crumbs, sticking in whole cloves. Bake slowly until well browned, basting at intervals with the juices. Do not carve until it is cold.

This is the way real Kentucky housekeepers cook Kentucky ham.

DESHA BRECKINRIDGE.

An ill cook should have a good cleaver.

Owen Meredith.

Belgian Hare

2 rabbits

1 quart sour cream

Thin slices of fat bacon

Skin rabbits and wash well in salt water. Cut off the surplus skin and use only the backs and hind quarters. Place in roasting pan, putting one slice of bacon on each piece of rabbit. Have the oven hot.

Start the rabbits cooking, turning the bacon over so it will brown; when brown turn down the gas to cook slowly. Pour ½ the cream over in the beginning and baste often. When half done pour in the remainder of the cream and cook 1½ hours.

If there is no sour cream, add 1 tablespoon of vinegar to sweet cream. The cream makes a delicious sauce.

Pepper Pot

Knuckle of Veal
4 lbs. Honey Comb tripe
1 Potato
1 Red Pepper
1 onion
A little summer savory
Sweet Basil

Soak tripe over night in salt water. Boil meat and tripe four to six hours.

Delicious Mexican Dish

Soak and scald a pair of sweetbreads, cut into small bits; take liquor from three dozen large oysters; add to sweetbreads with 3 tablespoons of gravy from the roast beef, and ¼ lb. of butter chopped and rolled in flour; cook until sweetbreads are tender; add oysters; cook 5 minutes; add ¾ cup of cream; serve with or without toast.

Hungarian Goulash

3 lbs. beef (cut in squares)
6 oz. bacon (cut in dice)
½ pint cream

4 oz. chopped onion

Cook onion and bacon; add salt and pepper; pour over them ½ pint water in which ½ teaspoon of extract of beef is added. Add the meat and cook slowly one hour; then add cream with paprika to taste and simmer for two hours. Add a few small potatoes.

Stewed Chicken

Clean and cut chicken and cover with water; add a couple sprigs of parsley; 1 bayleaf and a small onion. When chicken is almost done add salt and pepper to suit taste.

When chicken is done place in dish or platter and add one half cup cream to the gravy; thicken with a little blended flour and strain over chicken.

Chicken Pot Pie

Prepare same as for stewed chicken. When done remove chicken from bones; now boil potatoes enough for family. Line a deep baking dish or a deep pan with good rich paste. Sprinkle flour in bottom.

Lay in a layer of chicken; now potatoes, sprinkle with a little salt and pepper; now cut thin strips of dough, lay across; then a layer of chicken; then a layer of potatoes, and so on until the top of the pan is reached; pour over all the chicken, the gravy and put a crust over all the top and bake until well done and nicely browned.

Make little punctures in dough to allow the steam to escape.

Tell me what you eat, and I'll tell you what you are.—Brillat Savarin.

Anti's Favorite Hash

(Unless you wear dark glasses you cannot make a success of Anti's Favorite Hash.)

>1 lb. truth thoroughly mangled
>1 generous handful of injustice.
>(Sprinkle over everything in the pan)
>1 tumbler acetic acid (well shaken)

A little vitriol will add a delightful tang and a string of nonsense should be dropped in at the last as if by accident.

Stir all together with a sharp knife because some of the tid bits will be tough propositions.

—Ebensburg Mountaineer Herald.

Husband (Angrily) "Great guns! What are they Lamb Chops, Pork Chops or Veal Chops?"

Wife (serenely) "Can't you tell by the taste?"

He: "No, I can't, nor anybody else!"

She: "Well, then, what's the difference?"

Giblets and Rice

Boil 2 or 3 strings of chicken giblets (about 1 pound) until quite tender, drain, trim from bones and gristle and set aside.

Boil one cup rice in one quart water for fifteen minutes. Drain, put in double boiler with broth from giblets and let boil 1 hour. Brown 1 tablespoon flour in 1 tablespoon butter and 1 teaspoon sugar, add 1 chopped onion, and boiling water until smooth and creamy, then add some bits of chopped pickles or olives, salt, pepper, teaspoonful of vinegar and lastly giblets, cover and let simmer for twenty minutes. Put rice into a chop dish, serve giblets in the center. May be garnished with tomato sauce or creamed mushrooms or pimentos.

For a man seldom thinks with more earnestness of anything than he does of his dinner.

Sam'l Johnson

Savory Lamb Stew

Take two pounds spring lamb and braise light with butter size of a walnut. Add 3 cups boiling water, 3 onions, salt and pepper, and let simmer slowly for ½ hour. Then add six peeled raw potatoes and small head of young cabbage (cut in eighths) cover closely and allow at least an hour's slow boiling. This can be made on the stove, in the oven, or in fireless cooker.

The flavor of this dish can be varied by the addition of two or three tomatoes.

Squab Casserole

3 eggs boiled hard

1 teaspoon parsley, cut fine butter
seasoning to taste
1 teaspoon parmesan
a few little onions
few potato balls
bread crumbs

Clean the squab and dry thoroughly. Cut eggs fine, add parsley, parmesan cheese and seasoning. Now stuff each squab with this stuffing, putting a small piece of butter in each bird and sew up.

Place in a baking pan with a lump of butter and brown nicely on all sides. Now add a little water and cover and cook slowly until well done. While they are cooking add little onions and potato balls to the gravy.

I have sent but one recipe to a cook book, and that was a direction for driving a nail, as it has always been declared that women do not know how to drive nails. But that was when nails were a peculiar shape and had to be driven in particular way, but now that nails are made round there is no special way in which they need to be driven. So my favorite recipe cannot be given you.

As for my effort in the culinary line—I have not made an effort in the culinary line for more than at least thirty years, except once to make a clam pie, which was pronounced by my friends as very good. But I cannot remember how I made it. I have a favorite recipe, however, something of which I am very fond and which I might give to you. I got it out of the newspapers and it is as follows:

Spread one or two rashers of lean bacon on a baking tin, cover it thickly with slices of cheese, and sprinkle a little mustard and paprika over it. Bake it in a slow oven for half an hour and serve with slices of dry toast.

Now that is a particularly tasty dish if it is well done. I never did it, but somebody must be able to do it who could do it well.

Faithfully yours,
Anna H. Shaw.

Daube

Brown a thick slice from a round of beef in a hot pan and season carefully, adding water to make a pan gravy; add also a pint of tomato juice and onion juice to taste; cover and simmer gently for at least an hour and a half; turn the meat frequently, keeping the gravy in sufficient quantity to insure that the meat shall be thoroughly moist and thoroughly seasoned.

When served, it should be, if carefully done, very tender. The gravy may be thickened or not, according to individual taste.

Mrs. Sam'l Semple.

Liver a la Creole

Take a fine calf liver. Skin well and cut in thick slices. Season with salt and pepper. Fry in deep fat and drain.

Chop fine two tablespoons parsley. Melt two tablespoons butter, toss in parsley and pour at once over liver and serve.

Chicken Croquettes

1 pound of chicken

3 teaspoons chopped parsley
1½ cups cream
1 small onion
¼ pound butter
¼ pound bread crumbs
season to taste
1 pinch of paprika

Grind meat twice. Boil the onion with the cream and strain the onion out. Let cool and pour over crumbs. Add parsley and butter, and make a stiff mixture. Now add seasoning.

Mix all together by beating in the meat. If too thick add a little milk and form into croquettes, and put in ice box.

When cool dip in beaten egg and then in crackers or bread crumbs. Fry in deep fat.

Nuts as A Substitute for Meat

Although many are trying to eliminate so much meat from menus on account of its soaring cost, the person who performs hard labor must have in its place something which contains the chief constituents of meat, protein and fats, or the body will not respond to the demands made upon it because of lowered vitality from lack of food elements needed. Scientific analyses have proven that nuts contain more food value to the pound than almost any other food product known. Ten cent's worth of peanuts, for example, at 7 cents a pound will furnish more than twice the protein and six times more energy than could be obtained by the same outlay for a porterhouse steak at 25 cents a pound.

One reason for the tardy appreciation of the nutritive value of nuts is their reputation of indigestibility. The discomfort from eating them is often due to insufficient mastication and to the fact that they are usually eaten when not needed, as after a hearty meal or late at night, whereas, being so concentrated, they should constitute an integral part of the menu, rather than supplement an already abundant meal, says the Philadelphia Ledger. They should be used in connection with more bulky carbohydrate foods, such as vegetables, fruits, bread, crackers, etc.; too concentrated nutriment is often the cause of digestive disturbance, for a certain bulkiness is essential to normal assimilation.

Pecan Nut Loaf

1 cup hot boiled rice
1 cup pecan nut meat (finely chopped)
1 cup cracker crumbs

1 egg
1 cup milk
1¼ teaspoons salt
pepper to taste
1 teaspoon melted butter

Mix rice, nut meats, cracker crumbs; then add egg well beaten, the milk, salt and pepper.

Turn into buttered bread pan; pour over butter, cover and bake in a moderate oven 1 hour.

Put on hot platter and pour around same this sauce:

Cook 3 tablespoons butter with slice of onion and a few pimentos, stirring constantly. Add 3 tablespoons flour; stir, pour in gradually 1½ cups milk.

Season and strain.

"I am in earnest. I will not equivocate—I will not excuse—I will not retreat a single inch—AND I WILL BE HEARD."

Wm. Lloyd Garrison.

Nut Hash

Nut hash is a good breakfast dish. Chop fine cold boiled potatoes and any other vegetable which is on hand and put into buttered frying pan, heat quickly and thoroughly, salt to taste, and just before removing from the fire stir in lightly a large spoonful of peanut meal for each person to be served. To prepare the meal at home, procure raw nuts, shell them and put in the oven just long enough to loosen the brown skin; rub these off and put the nuts through the grinder adjusted to make meal rather than an oily mixture. This put in glass jars, and kept in a cool place will be good for weeks. It may too, be used for thickening soups or sauces, or may be added in small quantities to breakfast muffins and griddle-cakes.

Potato soup, cream of pea, corn or asparagus and bean soup may be made after the ordinary recipes, omitting the butter and flour and adding four tablespoons of peanut meal.

Nut Turkey

Nut turkey for Thanksgiving instead of the national bird, made by mixing one quart of sifted dry bread crumbs with one pint of chopped English walnuts—any other kind of nuts will go—and one cupful of peanuts, simply washed and dried, and adding a level teaspoon of sage, two of salt, a tablespoon of chopped parsley, two raw eggs, not beaten, and sufficient water to bind the mass together. Then form into the shape of a turkey, with pieces of macaroni to form the leg bones. Brush with a little butter and bake an hour in a slow oven and serve with drawn butter sauce.

A dinner roast made of nuts and cheese contains the elements of meat. Cook two tablespoons of chopped onion in a tablespoon of butter and a little water until it is tender, then mix with it one cupful each of grated cheese, chopped English walnuts and bread crumbs, salt and pepper to taste and the juice of half a lemon; moisten with water, using that in which the onion has been cooked; put into a shallow baking dish and brown in the oven.

Hickory nut loaf is another dish which can take the place of meat at dinner. Mix two cups of rolled oats, a cupful each of celery and milk, two cups of bread crumbs and two eggs, season and shape, then bake 20 minutes. Serve with a gravy made like other gravy, with the addition of a teaspoon of rolled nuts.

Nut Scrapple

On a crisp winter morning a dish of nut scrapple is very appetizing and just as nutritious as that made of pork. To make it, take two cupfuls of cornmeal, one of hominy and a tablespoon of salt and cook in a double boiler, with just enough boiling water until it is of the consistency of frying. While still hot add two cupfuls of nut meats which had been put through the chopper; pour into buttered pan and use like other scrapple.

Peanut omelet is a delicious way to serve nuts. Make a cream sauce with one tablespoon of butter, two tablespoons of flour and three-quarters of a cupful of flour and three-quarters of a cupful of milk poured in slowly.

Take from the fire, season, add three-quarters of a cupful of ground peanuts and pour the mixture on the lightly beaten yolks of three eggs. Fold in the stiffly beaten whites, pour into a hot baking dish and bake for 20 minutes.

Nut Roast

3 eggs (beaten with egg beater)
2 cups English Walnut meats
milk to moisten it
4 cups of bread crumbs (grated)
1 small tablespoon butter
pinch salt.

1½ cups of walnut meats will do. ¼ lb. of the meats is 1½ cups. A ¼ lb. of the meats equals ½ lb. in the shells and the labor of shelling is saved.

Melt butter and pour over mixture, salt, then add enough milk to moisten, so as to form the shape of a loaf of bread. Too little milk will cause the loaf to separate, likewise, too much will make it mushy. Chop walnuts exceedingly fine. Bake between 20 to 30 minutes in buttered bread pan or baking dish. A small slice goes very far as it is solid and rich. Serve with hot tomato sauce.

This makes a delicious luncheon dish, served with peas and a nice salad.

Oatmeal Nut Loaf

Oatmeal nut loaf can be served cold in place of meat for Sunday night tea. Put two cups of water in a sauce pan; when boiling add a cupful of oatmeal, stirring until thick; then stir in a cupful of peanuts that have been twice through the grinder, two tablespoons of salt, half a teaspoon of butter, and pack into a tin bucket with a tight fitting lid and steam for two hours; slice down when cold. This will keep several days if left in the covered tin and kept in a cool place. A delicious sandwich filling can be made from chopped raisins and nuts mixed with a little orange or lemon juice. Cooked prunes may be used instead of raisins.

Rastus: "So you wife am one of dem Suffragettes? Why don't yo show her de evil ob sech pernicious doctrine by telling her her place am beside de fireside?"

Sambo: "Huh! She dun shoot back sayin' dat if it wasn't foh her takin' in washin' dere wouldn't be any fireside."—Puck.

VEGETABLES

Cream Potatoes

Bake the potatoes in a slow oven. When perfectly cold slice rather thin. Put into a pan, sprinkle on a little flour and toss the potatoes about with your hand until some flour adheres to each piece. Cover these floured potatoes with small bits of butter. If the butter is put in in one piece the potatoes get broken before the butter reaches them all.

Sprinkle in a little salt and put in enough cream so that they are about half covered. If you use more cream they will cook too tender and be mushy before the cream is cooked down. Stand by them. Stir with a knife blade lifting them from the bottom but not turning them over.

When they begin to glisten lift them to a hot serving dish and put them where they will keep warm but will not cook any further.

If you have not cream add a little more butter but the cream is better than the butter.

HARRIET TAYLOR UPTON,
President, Ohio Women's Suffrage Association.
Warren, Ohio.

French Fried Potatoes

Wash and pare the potatoes and cut into any desired shape. Drain well. Fry in smoking fat until nicely browned, then drain on browned paper. Season well and serve.

Potatoes Au Gratin

Cut cold boiled potatoes into cubes and make a cream dressing. Butter the baking dish, put in a layer of potatoes and then a layer of the dressing, then sprinkle with a little parmesan cheese; now a layer of potatoes and then a layer of dressing and then cheese, put in oven and allow them to brown.

Potato Croquettes

Pare sweet or white potatoes and boil as for mashed potatoes. When done and mashed add a good lump of butter and season well; add a little hot milk, form into croquettes and dip into beaten egg, then in bread or cracker crumbs. Cook in deep fat. Garnish with parsley.

Let the sky rain potatoes.—Shakespeare

Pittsburgh Potatoes

1 onion
1 quart potato cubes
½ can pimentos
2 cups white sauce
½ lb. cheese
1 teaspoon salt

Cook potatoes with chopped onion. Drain and add pimentos cut fine. Pour white sauce over; stir in cheese; bake in a moderate oven.

Sweet Potato Souffle

Boil some sweet potatoes and ripe chestnuts separately, adding a little sugar to the water in which the chestnuts are boiled.

Mash all well together and add some cream and butter and beat until light. Then place for a minute or two in the oven to brown.

Potatoes a la Lyonnaise

Cut cold boiled potatoes into tiny dice of uniform size. Put two great spoonfuls of butter into the frying pan and fry two sliced onions in this for three minutes. With a skimmer remove the onions and turn the potatoes into the hissing butter. Toss and turn with a fork, that the dice may not become brown. When hot, add a teaspoon of finely chopped parsley and cook a minute longer. Remove the potatoes from the pan with a perforated spoon, that the fat may drip from them. Serve very hot.

Stuffed Potatoes

Wash good sized potatoes. Bake them and cut off tops with a sharp knife, and with a teaspoon scoop out the inside of each potato. Put this in a bowl with two ounces of butter, the yolks of two eggs, salt to taste, pepper and sugar.

Potato Dumplings

To be served with German Pot Roast or Beef a la mode.

4 large raw potatoes grated
8 large boiled potatoes grated
2 eggs
¾ cup bread crumbs
1 tablespoon melted butter

Mix eggs with grated raw potatoes, add bread crumbs and butter, lastly grated boiled potatoes and salt, mix flour with the hands while forming dumplings size of large egg, drop at once into boiling salted water.

Boil twenty minutes, drain, lay on platter and sprinkle with fried chopped onions, bread crumbs browned in butter.

Potato Puffers

Peel and grate 8 large potatoes, one onion, mix at once with two or three eggs (before potatoes have time to discolor). Have spider very hot with plenty of hot fat.

Drop into flat cakes 3 in. in diameter, fry crisp brown on one side then turn and fry second side. Serve immediately with apple sauce or stewed fruit of any kind.

Stuffed Tomatoes

(Luncheon Dish.)

5 large tomatoes
1 tablespoon minced green (sweet) peppers
minced onion
3 or 4 pork sausages
2 cups bread crumbs
1 teaspoon or tablespoon of minced parsley
salt and pepper
1 tablespoon melted butter

Boil the sausages ten minutes, then skin and chop fine. Hollow your tomatoes using about ½ cup of the solid parts, chopping fine. Mix all thoroughly then heap into the tomato shells. Put large tablespoon butter in baking pan and bake about 20 minutes in hot oven.

Green peppers and sausages can be omitted if so preferred.

This stuffed tomato served with bread and butter can be used as a first course instead of bouillon and also can be used as a substitute for meat.

Baked Tomatoes

8 large smooth tomatoes
2 green peppers
1 tsp. salt
1½ pints milk
1 good sized onion
1½ T. sugar
flour

Wash tomatoes, do not peel, slice piece from top of each and scoop out a little of the tomato. Cut peppers in two lengthwise and remove seeds—place in cold water.

Now put onion and peppers through meat chopper, sprinkle a little sugar and a little salt over each tomato and place in good sized baking dish; now put ground onion and ground peppers on top of tomato.

Put butter in skillet and when melted, not brown, stir in flour until a paste is formed, now add gradually the milk as you would for cream dressing, stir constantly.

The dressing must be very thick to allow for the water from the tomatoes. Put this sauce around the tomatoes, not on top and place in a moderate oven to bake about one hour slow. Serve if possible in the same dish in which it was baked as it is very attractive.

MARY ROBERTS RINEHART.

Green String Beans

¼ Peck

Fry in ham or bacon, 1 onion; add 1 cup tomatoes, 1 sprig thyme, 1 clove garlic—parsley. Add beans and 1 cup water. Cook 1½ hours.

Fresh Beans (Green or Yellow.)

¼ peck beans
1 good size onion
½ clove of garlic
2 small tomatoes
1 pinch of thyme
½ tablespoon butter
½ tablespoon bacon fat
Salt to taste

Cut beans lengthwise very thin. Put butter and bacon fat in saucepan. Cut up onion and let it fry to a light brown. Then wash beans and put them in the fat. Add garlic and tomatoes, (cut up) and thyme—a little salt and a little water. Cook.

Barbouillade

A dish from "fair Provence"

1 large or two small egg-plants; two cucumbers; four onions; six tomatoes; 1 green pepper.

Peel and cut separately all vegetables; fry sliced onions in a teaspoon of lard; add tomatoes, crushing them and stirring until quite soft; add half a teaspoon of salt, then the cucumber, egg-plant, and green pepper, stirring over a hot fire for ten minutes; place over a slow fire and stew for three hours.

If the vegetables are fresh and tender, nothing else is needed, but if they are somewhat dry, add a cupful of stock.

Cold barbouillade is excellent to spread on bread for sandwiches.

Barbouillade is usually served hot with rice boiled a la Creole.

Boiled Rice

Wash very thoroughly one cupful of rice; boil for twenty minutes in three quarts of boiling water; drain and shake well, pour cold water over the rice to separate the grains, and set in the oven a few minutes to keep hot.

Spinach

Wash thoroughly, then throw into cold water and bring to boiling point; then add ¼ teaspoon of soda and boil 5 minutes. Turn into colander, let cold water run over it, drain well, squeezing out water with spoon, then chop very fine; add creamed butter, salt and pepper.

Heat again thoroughly, then serve with hard boiled eggs sliced on top.

Spaghetti

½ box Spaghetti
1 can tomatoes
½ large onion
1 teaspoon salt
⅛ teaspoon pepper
3 tablespoons sugar
1 tablespoon flour
1 pint water
1 tablespoon butter
1½ lbs. boiling meat
Sap Sago or Parmesan cheese.

Boil spaghetti twenty-five minutes in salt water, drain, and run cold water over it to separate.

While the spaghetti is boiling make sauce as follows: put the butter in the skillet and when hot put in the onion and let brown. Then add the tomatoes, meat, water, salt, pepper, sugar and cook thoroughly for one and one-half hours. Then add flour mixed with a little water; thicken to the consistency of cream; strain.

Take baking dish and place a layer of spaghetti, then a layer of sauce, then sprinkle this with the cheese, continue until the pan is filled, allowing cheese to be on the top.

Bake one-half hour in a moderate oven.

Baked Beans

1 quart beans
1 scant teaspoon baking soda
3 tablespoons molasses
¼ pound salt pork

¼ pound bacon
3 tablespoons vinegar
½ teaspoon mustard
salt and pepper to taste
3 tablespoons catsup

Soak beans over night in luke warm water with soda. In morning pour off water and wash in cold water. Now place salt pork in bottom of bean crock and put layers of beans on top, sprinkle with pepper and salt, when filled nearly to top put on slices of bacon.

Now blend mustard with vinegar, now add molasses and catsup and pour over the beans and fill up and over the top with luke warm water. Bake in a slow oven for at least six hours, longer if necessary.

Creamed Mushrooms

1 lb. mushrooms
flour to thicken
¼ lb. butter
½ pt. sweet cream

To one pound of cleaned and well strained mushrooms, add ¼ lb. of fresh butter. Allow mushrooms to cook in butter about five minutes. Sprinkle enough flour to thicken.

When well mixed, pour in gently a little more than ½ pint of sweet cream. Allow it to boil, add salt and pepper to taste.

MRS. ENOCH RAUH.

Macaroni a la Italienne

2 lbs. ground meat
2 onions
1 large tablespoon butter
1½ tablespoons sugar
salt and pepper to taste

>1 large can tomatoes
>2 lbs. macaroni
>Parmesan cheese
>2, 3 or 4 cups water

Put butter in a pan and allow it to melt, add onions and cook until light brown, not dark. Now add meat and cook slowly, now add sugar, and seasoning and tomatoes, and as it cooks down add 1 cup of water. Allow it to cook three hours or longer, adding more water as it needs it. It will turn dark, almost a mahogany, as it nears the finishing point. When almost done put macaroni on in plenty of boiling salt water and cook almost twenty minutes. Do not allow it to cook entirely. When done drain off water. Now take baking dish, and put a layer of macaroni on bottom, now a layer of parmesan cheese, now a layer of the tomato and meat sauce, now a layer of cheese and repeat with macaroni, cheese, sauce, etc., until the top is reached. Put on a generous layer of sauce and cheese and allow it to bake about a half hour in a medium oven, being careful that it is not too hot.

Regarding how much water to add must be determined by cook. Some times it boils more rapidly. The sauce must not be too thin.

To serve with Macaroni Italienne the following is very fine.

Have the butcher cut a 2 pound round steak as thin as possible and prepare the following way:

>1 generous cup grated bread crumbs
>2 anchovies, cut fine
>½ tablespoon parsley, cut fine
>3 eggs boiled hard
>½ tablespoon parmesan cheese
>seasoning to taste

Grate the bread, cut anchovies and parsley fine. Mix all with seasoning and cheese and spread on steak. Now place the eggs which have been boiled hard, peel, and allow to remain whole on top of bread crumbs, etc. Place at equal distance from each other, and roll up and bind with skewers or cord. Put this into the pot with the tomato and meat sauce and allow it to cook until the sauce is done, at which time the meat roll will also be ready to serve. Place the roll on a dish and cut in slices.

This, with a light salad, is sufficient for a dinner.

Rice With Cheese

Cook a cup of rice in rapidly boiling, salted water until almost ready for the table. Drain, mix with a pint of white sauce, pour into a baking dish, cover with slices of cheese, and bake in a moderate oven twenty minutes.

The white sauce may also be flavored with cheese.

Rice With Nuts

Prepare rice as above, and mingle with white sauce; add half a cup of chopped nuts—pecans or hickory nuts preferred; sprinkle a few chopped nuts over surface, and brown in quick oven.

MRS. SAMUEL SEMPLE,
President, State Federation of Pennsylvania Women.

Carrot Croquettes

Boil four large carrots until tender; drain and rub through a sieve, add one cupful of thick white sauce, mix well and season to taste. When cold, shape into croquettes, and fry same as other croquettes.

Potato Balls

Two soup plates of grated potatoes which have been boiled in the skins the day before. Add four tablespoons flour or bread crumbs, a little nutmeg and salt, one-half cup of melted butter and the yolks of four eggs and one cupful croutons (fried bread—in butter—cut into small cubes).

Mix together, then add the beaten whites of the eggs. Mix well and form into balls, then boil in boiling salt water about fifteen or twenty minutes. Serve with bacon cut into small squares on top.

To be eaten with stewed dried fruits cooked together—prunes, apricots, apples.

MRS. RAYMOND ROBINS.

Vegetable Medley, Baked

To take the place of the roast on a meatless menu, try the following:

Soak and boil one-half pint of dried beans to make a pint of pulp, putting it through a colander to remove the skins. Take small can of tomato soup and to this allow a pint of nuts ground, two raw eggs, half a cup of flour browned, one small onion minced and a tablespoon of parsley, also minced. Season to taste with sage, sweet marjoram, celery salt, pepper and paprika and mix the whole well, stirring in half a cup of sweet milk. Put into a well-greased baking tin and brown for 20 minutes in a quick oven. Serve hot on a flat dish as you would a roast with brown gravy or tomato sauce.

Women cannot make a worse mess of voting than men have. They will make mistakes at first. That is to be expected. It will not be their fault, but the fault of the men who have withheld from them what they should have had before this. But eventually they will get their bearings, and will use the ballot to better effect than men have used it.

Whatever the outcome, it will be better to have intelligent women voting than the illiterates and incompetents who have now the right to the vote because they are men. We need to tighten up at one end of the voting question and broaden out at the other. We should take from the ignorant, worthless and unfit men who possess it, that right of suffrage which they do not know how to use. We should give to the thousands of intelligent women of the country the right of suffrage which should be theirs.

IRVIN S. COBB.

The waste of good materials, the vexation that frequently attends such mismanagement and the curses not unfrequently bestowed on cooks with the usual reflection, that whereas God sends good meat, the devil sends cooks. E. Smith.

SAVORIES

Hot savory and cold salad are always to be recommended—some suggestions that are worth remembering.

A hot savory and a cold salad make a good combination for the summer luncheon, and the savory is a useful dish for the disposition of left-over scraps of meat, fish, etc.

The foundation of a savory is usually a triangle or a finger or buttered brown bread toast, or fried bread, pastry or biscuit. The filling may be varied indefinitely, and its arrangement depends upon available materials.

Here are a few suggestions for the use of materials common to all households.

He that eats well and drinks well, should do his duty well.

Tomato Toast

Half an ounce of butter, two ounces of grated cheese, one tablespoon of tomato; paprika. Melt the butter and add the tomato (either canned or fresh stewed), then the grated cheese; sprinkle with paprika and heat on the stove. Cut bread into rounds or small squares, fry and pour over each slice the hot tomato mixture.

Ham Toast

Mince a little left-over boiled ham very finely. Warm it in a pan with a piece of butter. Add a little pepper and paprika. When very hot pile on hot buttered toast. Any left-over scraps of fish or meat may be used up in a similar way, and make an excellent savory to serve with a green salad.

Cheese Savories

Butter slices of bread and sprinkle over them a mixture of grated cheese and paprika. Set them in a pan and place the pan in the oven, leaving it there until the bread is colored, and the cheese set. Serve very hot.

Sardine Savories

Sardines, one hard boiled egg, brown bread, parsley. Cut the brown bread into strips and butter them. Remove the skin and the bones from the sardines and lay one fish on each finger of the bread. Chop the white of the egg into fine pieces and rub the yolk through a strainer. Chop the parsley very fine and decorate each sardine with layers of the white, the yolk and the chopped parsley. Season with pepper and salt.

Oyster Savories

These make a more substantial dish, and are delicious when served with a celery salad: Six oysters, six slices of bacon, fried bread, seasoning. Cut very thin strips of bacon that can be purchased already shaved is best for the purpose. Season the oysters with pepper and salt, and wrap each in a slice of the bacon, pinning it together with a wooden splint (a toothpick). Place each oyster on a round of toast or of fried bread, and cook in the oven for about five minutes. Serve very hot, and sprinkle with pepper.

Savory Rice and Tomato

Fry until crisp a quarter pound of salt pork. Put into the pan with it a medium sized onion, minced fine and brown. All this to three cupfuls of boiled rice; mix in two green peppers seeded and chopped, and a cupful of tomato sauce. Season all to taste with salt and pepper, turn into a buttered baking dish, sprinkle with fine breadcrumbs and small pieces of butter. Brown.

Stuffed Celery

A most delicious relish is made with Roquefort cheese, the size of a walnut, rubbed in with equal quantity of butter, moistened with sherry (lemon juice will serve if sherry be not available), and seasoned with salt, pepper, celery salt, and paprika; then squeezed into the troughs of a dozen slender, succulent sticks of celery. This is a very appropriate prelude to a dinner of roast duck.

JACK LONDON.

Here is bread which strengthens man's heart, and, therefore, is called the staff of life.   Mathew Henry

BREAD, ROLLS, ETC.

Fine Bread

3 small potatoes
1 tablespoon lard
2 handfuls salt
1 handful sugar

Soak the magic yeast cake in a little luke warm water. Add a little flour to this, and let it stand an hour. Boil the potatoes in 2 quarts water: when soft put through sieve and then set aside to cool in the potato water. Add to this the lard, salt and sugar.

About 4 in the afternoon put the liquid in large bread riser. Add about 3 quarts of flour, beat thoroughly for at least 10 minutes; now add dissolved yeast to it; let sponge rise until going to bed and then stiffen. Knead until dough does not stick to the hands about 20 to 25 minutes. It will double in size. In morning put in bread pans and let rise one hour or more. Bake in moderately hot oven one hour.

Many persons prefer stiffening the bread in the morning. In this case set the sponge later in the evening and allow it to rise all night, stiffening with the flour in the morning instead of the evening. Of course this allows the baking to be rather late in the day.

MRS. MEDILL MCCORMICK.

Excellent Nut Bread

Two cupfuls of white flour (sifted), two cupfuls of graham or entire wheat flour (sifted if one chooses), one-half cup of New Orleans molasses, little salt, two cupfuls of milk or water, one cupful of walnut meats (cut up fine), one teaspoonful of soda dissolved in milk, about two tablespoons melted butter. Let raise 20 minutes. Bake about one hour in moderate oven.

Virginia Batter Bread

2 cups milk
Salt to taste
1 tablespoon butter
½ cup of cream
½ cup white corn meal
2 to 5 well beaten eggs

Put in double boiler 2 cups of milk and ½ cup of cream. When this reaches boiling point salt to taste. While stirring constantly sift in ½ cup of white corn meal (this is best). Boil 5 minutes still stirring, then add 1 tablespoon of butter and from 2 to 5 well beaten eggs (beaten separately) 1 for each person is a good rule.

Pour into a greased baking dish and bake in a quick oven until brown like a custard. It must be eaten hot with butter and is a good breakfast dish.

Mrs. K. W. Barrett.

Bran Bread

4 cups sterilized bran
2 cups buttermilk
raisins if desired
2 cups white flour
½ teaspoon soda

Bake until thoroughly done.

Editress Suffrage Cook Book:

I take pleasure in sending you a portrait and also my favorite recipe for food, which I hope will be of some use to you and help the cause along.

Mush should be made only of the whole meal flour of the grain and well cleaned before grinding. Whole wheat flour, whole Indian Corn Meal, whole wheat and whole barley meal are examples of the raw materials.

Take one pint (pound) of meal, ½ teaspoon of salt, four pints (pounds) of water. Add the salt to the water and after boiling stir in slowly, so as to avoid making lumps, the meal until all is used. Break up any lumps that may form with the ladle until the mass is homogeneous.

Cover the vessel and boil slowly over a low fire so as not to burn the contents, for an hour. Or better after bringing to a boil in a closed vessel place in a fireless cooker over night.

This is the best breakfast food that can be had and the quantity above mentioned is sufficient for from four to six persons. The cost of the raw material based on the farmer's price is not over 1½ cents.

Variation: Mush may also be made with cold water by careful and continuous stirring. There is some advantage of stirring the meal in cold water as there is no danger of lumping but without very vigorous stirring especially at the bottom, the meal may scorch during the heating of the water.

The food above described is useful especially for growing children as the whole meal or flour produce the elements which nourish all the tissues of the body.

Respectfully,
Dr. Harvey W. Wiley.

Dr. Wiley urges house wives to grind their own wheat flour and corn meal, using the coffee grinder for the work. The degree of fineness of flour is regulated by frequent grindings.

The improvement in flavor and freshness of cakes, breads and mush made from home ground wheat and corn will absolutely prove a revelation.

Polenta—Corn Meal

Take an iron kettle, put in two quarts water with one tablespoon salt. Heat and before boiling, slowly pour in your corn meal, stirring continuously until you have it very stiff. Put on lid and let boil for an hour or more. Turn out in a pan and keep warm. Later this is turned out on a platter for the table.

Cut it in pieces of about an inch wide for each plate and on this the following sauce is added with a teaspoon Parmesan cheese added to each piece.

Brown a good sized onion in two tablespoons butter, add ½ clove of garlic, about 5 pieces of dried mushroom, being well soaked in water (use the water also) dissolve a little extract of beef, pouring that into this with a little more water, salt and some paprika—a pinch of sugar and $1/3$ teaspoon vinegar.

A little flour to make a nice gravy. This makes it very palatable.

It takes about ten minutes to cook.

Serve in gravy bowl—a spoonful on each piece of Polenta. Added to that the grated cheese, is all that is needed for a whole meal. Apple sauce should be served with this dish.

Man doth not live by bread alone.

—Owen Meredith

Corn Bread

1 pint corn meal
1 pint flour
1 teaspoon soda
2 teaspoons cream of tartar
1 teaspoon salt
1 tablespoon sugar
¼ cup melted butter
1 pint milk
1 egg

Mix the dry ingredients together. Bake in rather quick oven.

Nut Bread

1 beaten egg
1½ cups sweet milk
1 cup light brown sugar
1 cup nuts (Chop before measuring)
4 cups flour
4 teaspoons baking powder

Let rise 30 minutes. Bake one hour.

Hymen Bread

1 lb. genuine old love
⁷/₈ lb. common sense
¾ lb. generosity
½ lb. toleration
½ lb. charity
1 pinch humor

(always to be taken with a grain of salt.)

Good for 365 days in the year.

Corn Bread

1 cup flour
2 cups corn meal (yellow)
½ cup sugar
3 teaspoons baking powder
¼ teaspoon salt
2 eggs
2 cups milk

1 tablespoon butter

Sift all dry ingredients—sugar, flour, meal, salt and baking powder.

Beat yolks and add milk, stir into dry materials. Now beat whites stiff and add. Lastly stir in melted butter. Bake in greased pans about twenty to thirty minutes.

Brown Bread

1 cup sweet milk
½ cup brown sugar
1 teaspoon salt
Graham flour to make a stiff batter
1 cup sour milk
½ cup molasses
1 small teaspoon baking soda

Bake 1 hour and a quarter in a moderate oven. Stir in soda, dissolved, last thing, beating well. This makes 2 small loaves.

Egg Bread

1 quart meal
1 teaspoon salt
3 eggs
1 cup milk
1 tablespoon lard and butter

Pour a little boiling water over 1 quart of meal to scald it. Add a little salt and stir in yolks of 3 eggs, 1 cup milk, 1 tablespoon of lard and butter melted. Add the whites last, well beaten.

Bake in a moderate oven till well done—almost an hour.

Quick Waffles

2 eggs
1 quart of milk
1 quart of flour
a little salt
1 tablespoon molten butter
1 teaspoon sugar

Beat the eggs very light; then gradually mix in the milk, flour and salt; add melted butter.

Pour into the waffle iron and bake at once.

Grease irons well and do not put in too much batter.

Dumplings That Never Fall

Two cupfuls of flour, two heaping teaspoons of baking powder, one-half teaspoon of salt and one cupful of sweet milk. Stir and drop in small spoonfuls into plenty of water, in which meat is boiling. Boil with cover off for fifteen minutes, then put cover on and boil ten minutes longer. These are very fine with either beef or chicken.

STATE OF ARIZONA
EXECUTIVE MANSION

Since equal suffrage became effective in Arizona in December, 1912, the many critics of the innovation have been quite effectually silenced by the advantageous manner in which enfranchisement of women has operated. Not only have the women of this state evinced an intelligent and active interest in governmental issues, but in several instances important offices have been conferred upon that element of the electorate which recently acquired the elective franchise. Kindly assure your co-workers in Pennsylvania of my best wishes for their success.

W. P. HUNT.
Governor.

French Rolls

3 eggs
3 ounces butter
1 quart of flour
1 pint sweet milk
1 cake yeast
a little salt

Beat the eggs very light; melt the butter in the milk; add a little flour and a little milk until all is mixed; then add yeast before all the milk and flour are added.

Make into rolls and bake in a pan.

This should be made up at night and set to rise, and baked the next morning.

Drop Muffins

3 eggs
1 quart of milk
1 tablespoon butter
¾ cake yeast
flour to make a batter stiff enough for a spoon to stand upright.

Make up at night and in morning drop from spoon into pan. Bake in a quick oven.

We'll bring your friends and ours to this large dinner. It works the better eaten before witnesses.

—Cartwright.

Soft Gingerbread

½ cup butter
2 eggs
1 cup hot water
1 teaspoon cloves
1 teaspoon soda
½ cup sugar
1 teacup molasses
1 teaspoon cinnamon
1 teaspoon ginger
2½ cups flour

Dissolve soda in couple teaspoonfuls hot water.

Gingerbread

1 cup sugar
1 cup molasses
2½ cups flour
¾ cups lard and butter
2 eggs
1 dessert spoon soda dissolved in cup cold water

1 teaspoon ginger
1 teaspoon cloves
1 teaspoon cinnamon

Bake in slow oven and leave in pan until cold.

Cream Gingerbread

2 eggs, beaten, add
¾ cup sugar
¾ cup sour milk
1 tablespoon ginger
¾ cup molasses
1 teaspoon cinnamon
1½ level teaspoon soda well sifted
2 level cups flour

Bake in gem pans. Greatly improved by adding nuts and raisins.

Cream Gingerbread Cakes

2 eggs
½ cup molasses
grated rind of ½ lemon
1 teaspoon cinnamon
2 cups flour
½ cup sugar
¾ cup thick sour milk
1 saltspoon salt
1 tablespoon ginger
1½ teaspoons soda (level)

Beat 2 eggs until light, add ½ cup of sugar, ½ cup molasses, ¾ cup thick sour cream, the grated rind of ½ lemon, 1 saltspoon of salt, 1 teaspoon cinnamon, 1 tablespoon ginger, and finally, add 2 cups of well sifted flour mixed with 1½ teaspoons soda (level).

Bake in gem pans. If desired add nuts and raisins which improves them very much.

Parliament Gingerbread

(With apologies to the English Suffragists)

½ lb. flour
½ lb. treacle
1 oz. butter
½ small spoon soda

1 dessert spoon ginger
1 dessert spoon mixed spices
½ cup sugar

A bit of hot water in which soda is dissolved.

Put flour in a basin, and rub in butter, and dry ingredients; then, soda and water; pour in treacle, and knead to smooth paste. Roll quite thin and cut in oblongs. Bake about ¼ hour.

Soft Gingerbread

1 cup sour milk
½ cup butter
2 eggs
2 pints flour
1 cup molasses
½ cup sugar
1½ teaspoons soda
2 teaspoons ginger

Dr. Van Valja's Griddle Cakes

1 cup boiled rice
1 level tablespoon flour
yolks of three eggs
pinch salt

Beat the eggs to a froth, put in the rice and flour, bake on rather hot griddle greased with butter—eat with sugar and cinnamon.

Very good for a dyspeptic.

Sally Lunn

¼ cup sugar
1 egg
2 cups flour
2 tablespoons melted butter
1 cup milk
3 teaspoons baking powder

A good breakfast toast is made by dipping the slices of bread in a pint of milk to which a beaten egg and a pinch of salt are added, and frying.

When Heat Turns Milk Sour

Here is a sour cream filling for cake: Mix equal quantities of thick, sour cream, chopped nuts and raisins. Add a little sugar and lemon juice, enough to give the proper taste, and spread between layers of cake.

Many kinds of cookies can be made with sour milk. Here is the recipe for a good sort: Cream half a cup of butter with a cup of sugar and add a cup of sour milk in which three-quarters of a teaspoon of soda has been dissolved, and two cups or a little more of flour, sifted with half a teaspoon of cloves, half a teaspoon of cinnamon and a teaspoon of salt. Chill the dough before cutting the cookies. It must be rolled thin.

Corn bread can be made with sour milk in this way: Sift a cup of cornmeal with half a cup of flour, half a teaspoon of salt, a tablespoon of shortening (clear chicken fat that has been fried out is a good kind), and then add a cupful of sour milk and a beaten egg. Lastly, add half a teaspoon of soda. It is well to add the soda last, where a light mixture is desired, as it begins to give off carbon dioxide, the gas that makes the dough rise, as soon as it is moist and comes in contact with the acid of the sour milk.

Graham bread made with sour milk in this way is delicious: Sift together a cup and a half of graham flour and one of white. Add a cup of broken nut meats and a teaspoon of salt. Then stir in half a cup of milk and a cup and a half of sour milk, and, lastly, add a teaspoon of soda. The soda may be sifted into a little of the white flour and added last, if adding it with the flour is easier.

CAKES, COOKIES, TARTS, ETC.

Mocha Tart

Beat the yolks of four eggs with 1 cup sugar to a cream, to which add 1 tablespoon of mocha extract (Cross and Blackwell's). Beat whites stiff and fold them in with ¾ cup of flour and 1 teaspoon baking powder. Bake in 2 layers in oven.

Filling for Mocha Tart

¾ pint cream well whipped, to which add 1½ tablespoons mocha extract. Sugar to taste. Ice top with boiled icing flavored with one tablespoon of mocha extract.

Icing

1 coffee cup sugar
2 Eggs
2 tablespoons butter
2 lemons (juice)

Beat all together and boil until it jellies. For orange cake use oranges instead of lemons.

Filling

1 Lemon
1 cup Water
½ cup Sugar
1 tablespoon Corn Starch
1 Egg
Grated lemon rind
1 teaspoonful butter

Icing

3 cups brown sugar
1 cup sweet milk
3 large tablespoons butter

Boil until it will make a ball in cold water. Then beat until thick enough to spread on cake. Flavor with vanilla.

Filling for Cake

3 grated apples

1 cup sugar
1 egg

Juice and grated rind of an orange or lemon. Let it come to a boil.

Delicious Nut Cake

Old English Recipe, year 1600

Coffee cup is used for measure.

2 cups of sugar rolled fine or sifted
1 cup of butter—creamed together
3 cups of flour—sifted 4 times
1 cup of cold water
4 eggs, whites and yolks beaten separately
2 large cups of walnut chopped or rolled
2 teaspoons of cream of tartar—level measure

Cream butter and sugar, stir in yolks, beat hard for 5 minutes, add water, then flour, mix the tartar in it—then nuts, then beaten whites of eggs. Bake ¾ of an hour if loaf, or half hour if divided into two portions or layers.

Icing

4 cups sugar
½ pint hot water
4 eggs beaten
citric acid about size of pea
vanilla

Boil water and sugar until it threads. Pour over the beaten whites of 4 eggs. Beat until almost cold then add citric acid dissolved in one teaspoon boiling water, flavor with vanilla and spread between layers and over cake.

This keeps a long time in a locked closet.

Cookery has become an art, a noble science; cooks are gentlemen.

Burton.

Christmas Cakes

½ lb. Butter
6 Eggs
1 lb. Powdered Sugar
Flour enough to roll

Beat eggs separate

Cream butter; add sugar. Separate eggs; beat and add. Then flour to roll.

Cocoanut Tarts

7 eggs (whites)
1 lb. sugar (pulverized)
½ lb. butter
1 cocoanut

Grate the cocoanut, beat the butter and sugar to a cream; beat the eggs until very dry and light; mix well together and bake on pie crusts rolled very thin. This amount will make four large tarts.

Suffrage Angel Cake

(a la Kennedy)

11 eggs
1 full cup Swansdown Flour (after sifting)
1½ cups granulated sugar
1 heaping teaspoon cream of tartar
2 teaspoons vanilla
1 pinch of salt

Beat the eggs until light—not stiff; sift sugar 7 times, add to eggs, beating as little as possible. Sift flour 9 times, using only the cupful, discarding the extra flour; then put in the flour the cream of tartar; add this to the eggs and sugar; now the vanilla. Put in angel cake pan with feet. Put in oven with very little heat. Great care must be used in baking this cake to insure success. Light the oven when you commence preparing material. After the first 10 minutes in oven, increase heat and continue to do so every five minutes until the last 4 or 5 minutes, when strong heat must be used. At thirty minutes remove cake and invert pan allowing to stand thus until cold.

MISS ELIZA KENNEDY.

Cinnamon Cake

1 cake compressed Yeast
¼ lb. Butter
1 tablespoon lard
1½ cups sugar
Pinch of Salt
1 pint luke warm milk
Flour to stiffen

About six o'clock in the evening soak a cake of yeast in a little luke warm water, make sponge with a little flour, water and yeast. Let rise until light, about an hour.

Melt butter and lard and cream with sugar and salt; add luke warm milk and some flour, then stir in sponge and gradually add more flour until stiff, not as stiff as bread dough. Do not knead, simply stiffen.

Let rise until morning, then simply put in square or round cake pans about one and one-half inches thick. Do not roll, just mold with the hands and let rise about an hour.

Cover with little lumps of butter, then sprinkle with sugar and cinnamon and bake twenty minutes. Thin slices of apples can be placed on top, also peaches or almonds, blanched and chipped.

This is the genuine German cinnamon cake, and is excellent.

Inexpensive Spice Cake

½ cup shortening
2 cups brown sugar
grated rind of lemon
2 eggs, 3 cups flour
1 lb. seeded raisins
½ teaspoon cinnamon
dash of cloves and nutmeg

Boil raisins in 1½ cups water twenty minutes.

Mix shortening, sugar, lemon rind, eggs and spices, add one cup flour then raisins drained but still hot. Then the other two cups flour and ½ cup of the water in which the raisins were boiled to which add 1 teaspoon bi-carbonate soda.

Bake in gem pans in moderate oven. This makes 30 cakes which can be iced with white or chocolate icing.

Black Walnut Cake

1 cup butter (creamed)
1 cup sugar
4 eggs
1 cup milk
2 teaspoons baking powder
Flour to stiffen
1 cup walnuts
1 teaspoon vanilla

Bake 20 or 30 minutes according to oven.

Scripture Cake

1 cup of	butter—Judges 5	chap. 25	Verse
3½ " "	flour—1 Kings 4	" 22	"
3 " "	sugar—Jeremiah 6	" 20	"
2 " "	raisins—1 Sam'l 30	" 12	"
2 " "	figs—1 Sam'l 30	" 12	"
1 " "	water—Genesis 24	" 17	"
1 " "	almond—Genesis 43	" 11	"
	6 eggs—Isaiah 10	" 14	"
1 tablespoon of	Honey—Exodus 33	" 3	"
A pinch of	salt—Leviticus 2	" 13	"
Spices to	taste—1 Kings 10	" 10	"

Follow Solomon's advice for making good boys, and you will have a good cake.

Proverbs: 23 Ch. 14 Verse.

STATE OF CALIFORNIA
EXECUTIVE MANSION

Since its adoption in October, 1911, equal suffrage in California has been put to the most thorough and severe test. Every conceivable sort of election has been held in the past three years, and women have been called upon to exercise their new privilege and perform their added duty not alone in the usual fashion, but in various primaries, including one for presidential preference, in local option elections, and they have been compelled to pass on laws and governmental policies presented to the electorate by the initiative and referendum.

The women have met the test and equal suffrage in California has fully justified itself. In nineteen eleven, by a very narrow margin the amendment carried.

Were it to be again submitted, the vote in its favor would be overwhelming.

HIRAM JOHNSTON,
Governor.

Ratan Kuchen

½ lb. butter
1 pint milk
4 eggs
1 cake yeast
¾ cup seedless raisins
¼ pound blanched almonds (split)
1 cup sugar
1 pinch salt

Soak yeast in a little warm water and some of the milk 10 minutes, then set a sponge and let it stand about 1 hour (before breakfast); cream butter; add sugar and beat thoroughly; beat the 4 eggs light and add gradually to creamed butter and sugar; now add the other ½ pint of milk.

Beat well and add the raisins, dredge with a little flour; now add sponge and beat all thoroughly for ½ hour till it drops from the spoon a little thicker than a sweet cake.

Grease your pan with butter and take the split almonds and stick them on the side of the pan. Bake nearly an hour.

This makes 2 small cakes or one large one. Very fine German Coffee Cake. You should use a pan with a tube in the center.

Golden Cake

½ cup butter
1 cup sugar
Yolks 10 eggs
½ cup milk
2 cups flour
3 teaspoons baking powder
2 teaspoons orange extract
cream butter

Add sugar gradually and yolks of eggs beaten until thick, add lemon colored extract. Mix and sift flour and baking powder and add alternately with milk to first mixture.

Pineapple Cake

1 egg
½ cup butter
¾ cup sugar
¾ cup milk
1½ teaspoons baking powder
1½ cups flour

Make in two layers and when ready to serve put grated pineapple on each layer of cake. Whip half a pint of cream, sweeten to taste and put over pineapples.

(Bananas can be used instead of pineapples).

Ginger Cookies

3 lbs. flour
1 lb. butter and lard mixed
1 lb. brown sugar
1 pint molasses
1 good sized teaspoon of soda or 2 level ones.

Add ginger to taste—about 4 level teaspoons, also lemon extract or grated rind and juice if preferred.

Put flour, sugar and butter together and rub thoroughly. Make hole in center and pour in the molasses in which the soda has been beaten in. Stir all well together, break off enough to roll out; cut, space in pan and bake in very moderate oven.

These keep well, especially in stone crock. This recipe makes a quantity if cut with small cutter.

Pound Cake

1 lb. flour
1 lb. pulverized sugar
flavoring
1 lb. butter
10 eggs

Cream butter and sugar to finest possible consistency. Add ¼ of the flour and beat well. Have eggs beaten to a froth. Add a few tablespoons at a time and beat thoroughly after each addition of egg. When eggs are all in, add balance of flour and flavoring and beat.

Bake in a slow oven one and one-half hours.

Hints:—Secret of fine pound cake is in the mixing, much beating being essential.

One-half the recipe serves fifteen persons amply.

A paler yellow cake can be had by substituting the whites of two eggs for every yolk discarded.

In the full recipe not more than four yolks should be discarded.

A very little lemon combined with vanilla or almond, improves the flavor of the cake.

Bake, if possible, in an old-fashioned tin pan with a center tube.

Doughnuts

1 cup Sugar
2 Eggs
2 tablespoons melted butter
1 cup sour or butter milk
1 small teaspoon soda
Flour enough to make a soft dough

1 teaspoon baking powder

Mix eggs, sugar and butter; add sour milk or buttermilk with soda dissolved. Then stir in flour with baking powder added.

Do not roll too thin.

Have lard boiling when you drop in the doughnuts. A slice of raw potato in the lard will prevent the lard taste.

Cream Cake

1 Cup Butter
1 tablespoon Lard
2 cups Sugar
1 cup Sweet Milk
3 Eggs
2 teaspoons Baking Powder
1 teaspoon Vanilla
1 Quart Flour

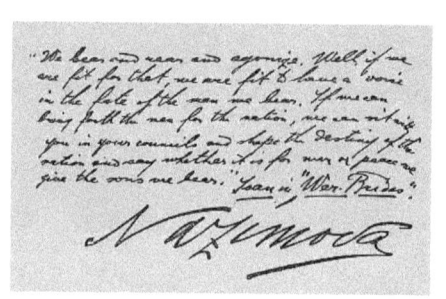

To aid the reader, a larger image of the handwritten note can be found by clicking on this image.

- 62 -

One Egg Cake

1 cup butter
1½ cups sugar
3 cups flour
1 cup sweet milk
1 egg
3 teaspoons baking powder
1 cup chopped raisins

Devil's Food

2 cups brown sugar
2 eggs
3 cups flour
½ cup boiling water
½ cup sour cream
½ cup butter
½ cup grated chocolate
1½ teaspoons soda

Dissolve soda in boiling water and pour over chocolate and let cool. Beat butter and sugar to a cream, add the eggs and other things. Bake in layers.

Bride's Cake

12 eggs (whites)
1 small cup butter
4 small cups flour
2 teaspoons baking powder
3 cups sugar
1 cup sweet milk
½ cup corn starch
Flavor to taste

This makes two good sized cakes, or four layers.

Date Cake

1 Cup Sugar
½ Cup Butter
2 Eggs
2 Cups Flour
1 heaping teaspoon baking powder
1/3 cup Milk

1 lb. stoned and chopped dates rolled on a portion of the flour

Cream the sugar and butter. Add the well beaten yolks; then the whites; then the flour well sifted with the baking powder. Beat until smooth; add milk, then dates. Beat thoroughly and bake three-quarters of an hour in a steady, but not too hot oven.

Pfeffernusse (Pepper Nuts)

1 cup Lard
1 cup Butter
2 cups Brown Sugar
3 Eggs
2 teaspoons Annise seed (ground)
2 oz. whole coriander seed
½ lb. Chopped Almonds
½ lb. Mixed Citron
6 cups Molasses
2 teaspoons Soda
1 Quart Flour
1 teaspoon Cream of Tartar

Cocoanut Cake

1 cup butter
1 cup sweet milk
1 teaspoon soda
1 grated cocoanut
3 cups sugar
4½ cups flour
2 teaspoons cream tartar
4 eggs (beaten separately)

In place of the soda and cream of tartar 3 teaspoons of baking powder can be used.

Jam Cake

1 cup brown sugar
2-3 cup butter and lard
3 eggs
1 glass of strawberry jam
1 teaspoon cloves
1 teaspoon cinnamon
½ grated nutmeg
½ cup sour milk

1 teaspoon soda
2 cups flour

Bake in a slow oven.

A march before day to dress one's dinner, and a light dinner to prepare one's supper are the best cooks.   Alexander.

Hickory Nut Cake

1 cup sugar
½ cup sweet milk
3 eggs
½ cup butter
2 teaspoons baking powder
flour to stiffen

One large cup chopped hickory nuts and sprinkle a little salt and flour with them. This makes two layers.

Lace Cakes

1 cup brown sugar
1 egg, not beaten
1½ tablespoon flour
1 round teaspoon butter
1 cup English walnuts chopped

Bake on the underside of a pan in a slow oven. This makes 20 cakes.

"Do not misunderstand me. Woman suffrage is right. It is just. It is expedient. In all moral issues the woman voters make a loyal legion that cannot be betrayed to the forces of evil; and however they are betrayed—as we all are—in campaigns against the Beast, the good that they do in an election is a great gain to a community and a powerful aid to reform. I believe that when the women see the Beast, they will be the first to attack it. I believe that in this our first successful campaign against it, the women saved us."

HON. BEN LINDSAY.

Lace Cakes

1 cup sugar
1 teaspoon butter
2 teaspoons baking powder
1 teaspoon vanilla
2 eggs
2½ cups rolled oats

Cream butter, add sugar and eggs. To this add vanilla and baking powder, and when these are thoroughly mixed, stir in the oats. This should make a stiff batter, and more oats may be added if batter is not stiff enough.

Mold into little cakes with a teaspoon and bake in buttered pans two inches apart, for ten minutes.

Marshmallow Teas

Arrange marshmallows on thin, unsweetened round crackers. Make a deep impression in center of each marshmallow, and in each cavity drop ¼ teaspoon butter. Bake until marshmallows spread and nearly cover crackers. After removing from oven insert half a candied cherry in each cavity.

These are excellent with afternoon tea.

Apple Sauce Cake

½ cup butter
a little salt
3 cups sifted flour
½ teaspoon cloves
½ cup nuts
1½ cups apple sauce
1½ cups sugar
½ teaspoon cinnamon
1 cup seeded raisins
2 scant teaspoons soda dissolved in a little water, boiling.

Bake in a slow oven.

Quick Coffee Cakes

Cream one-fourth of a cupful of butter, three-fourths of a cupful of sugar, one egg; add one cupful of milk, two and one-half cupfuls of flour in which two teaspoons of baking powder have been sifted. Beat smooth, then add as many raisins as desired and bake in two pie tins. When the top has begun to crust over, brush with melted butter and sprinkle with sugar and cinnamon. Bake a golden brown.

Sand Tarts

One pound of granulated sugar, three-quarters of a pound of butter, one pound of flour, one pound of almonds blanched and split, and three eggs. Cream butter and sugar till very light, add the yolks of the three eggs and the whites of two. Add the flour; roll on the board and cut in oblong or diamond shapes. Beat the white of the remaining egg and bake.

Sand Tarts

2 lbs. light brown sugar
¾ lb. butter
2 lbs. flour
3 eggs

Milk enough to make a stiff dough. Roll very thin, cut out and brush over with beaten egg and milk mixed together. Put two or three blanched almonds on each tart and dust with cinnamon and sugar.

Bake in moderate oven.

Cheap Cake

2 cups sugar
1 teaspoon butter
4 cups flour

3 eggs
1 cup water
2 teaspoons baking powder
Flavor to taste

THE STATE OF WYOMING
EXECUTIVE DEPARTMENT
Cheyenne.

Dec. 22, 1914.

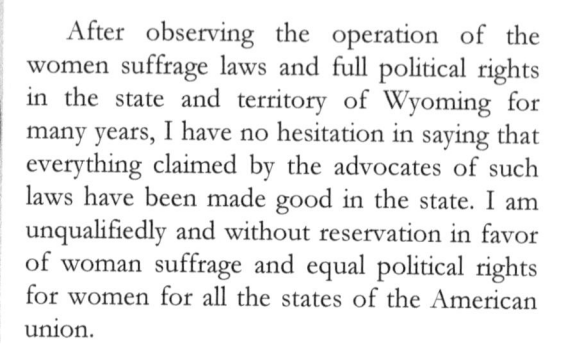

Editress Suffrage Cook Book:

After observing the operation of the women suffrage laws and full political rights in the state and territory of Wyoming for many years, I have no hesitation in saying that everything claimed by the advocates of such laws have been made good in the state. I am unqualifiedly and without reservation in favor of woman suffrage and equal political rights for women for all the states of the American union.

Very truly yours,
JOSEPH M. CAREY.
Governor.

Hermits

1½ cups sugar
¾ cup butter
3 tablespoons milk—sweet or sour
3 eggs—whites and yolks beaten separately
1 teaspoon soda
1 heaping teaspoon cinnamon
1 heaping teaspoon ginger
1 level teaspoon cloves
1 cup chopped seeded raisins

1 cup chopped nuts
Even cup of flour

Drop on greased pan and bake.

Hermits

1½ cups sugar
3 eggs
1 cup chopped walnuts or hickory nuts
1 teaspoon cinnamon
1 teaspoon vanilla
1 cup butter
1 cup chopped raisins
1-3 cup sliced citron
1 teaspoon cloves
½ teaspoon soda

Dissolve soda in tablespoon hot water. Flour enough to make a stiff batter, drop in small cakes with teaspoon and bake in slow oven.

Cocoanut Cookies

1 cup butter
4 eggs
1 lemon—juice and rind
4 cups sugar
4 teaspoons baking powder
1 pound package grated cocoanut

Cream sugar with butter. Add the yolks of the 4 eggs and beat well. Add juice and rind of lemon. Then flour, into which has been sifted the baking powder. Sift flour and baking powder twice before adding to mixture. Use enough flour to make a very stiff batter, add cocoanut, and last, fold in the whites of the eggs beaten to a stiff froth.

Drop on buttered tins and bake in moderate oven.

PASTRIES, PIES, ETC.

Grape Fruit Pie

First bake a shell as for lemon pie, then make a filling as follows: Mix one tablespoon of cornstarch in a little cold water, and over this pour one cupful of boiling water. To this add the juice of two grapefruits, the grated rind and juice of one orange, the beaten yolks of two eggs, and the white of one, and a small piece of butter. Put all in the double boiler and cook until thick, stirring all the time. When done, put in the shell. Now beat up the white of the second egg with one-half a cupful of sugar until thick, and spread with a knife over the pie. Put in the oven and let brown lightly. Serve cold. This makes a delicious pie.

Spice Pie

The yolks of three eggs, one and one-half cupfuls of sugar, one cupful of cream, two tablespoons of flour, two-thirds of a cupful of butter, one teaspoon of spice, cloves, cinnamon and nutmeg.

Mix the flour and sugar together, then cream with the butter. Add the yolks of the eggs, beating thoroughly. Next add cream and spices. Use the whites for the frosting.

Cream Pie

1½ cups milk
2 egg yolks
2 tablespoons sugar
a little salt
1 tablespoon butter
Vanilla to taste

Scald milk; beat eggs; add sugar; pour into milk, beating constantly, 1 tablespoon of cornstarch and 1 tablespoon flour (rounded).

Bake crust; beat whites; add 1 teaspoon sugar, cover with cocoanut browned lightly; now cover with whipped cream and cream nuts.

Pie Crust

One level cup of flour, one-half cup of lard, one-half teaspoon salt, one-fourth cup ice cold water, one teaspoon baking powder. Mix salt, baking powder and flour thoroughly, chop in the lard, add water. Use as little flour as possible when rolling out. This makes a light, crisp, flaky and delicious pie crust.

Pie for a Suffragist's Doubting Husband

    1 qt. milk human kindness
    8 reasons:
    War
    White Slavery
    Child Labor
    8,000,000 Working Women
    Bad Roads
    Poisonous Water
    Impure Food

Mix the crust with tact and velvet gloves, using no sarcasm, especially with the upper crust. Upper crusts must be handled with extreme care for they quickly sour if manipulated roughly.

Sigmund Spaeth, in his "Operatic Cook Book, in Life," gives this recipe for the making of the opera "Pagliacci."

Beat a large bass drum with the white of one clown. Then mix with a prologue and roll very thin. Fill with a circus just coming to town. One leer, one scowl and one tragical grin. Bake in a sob of Carusian size. Result: the most toothsome of Italy's pies.

Where is the man that can live without dining?

                                                       —Lytton.

Orange Pie

    1 Large Grated Apple
    1 Orange—grated rind and juice
    ½ cup Sugar
    2 Eggs—Butter size of an egg

  Grate apple; add orange, sugar, butter and yolks. Beat whites and add lastly. Bake slowly in open shells.

Lancaster County Pie

    1 cup molasses
    1 teaspoon soda
    1 cup sugar
    1 cup boiling water
    3 cups flour

½ cup butter

Make a pie crust and line 4 pie pans. Put soda in the molasses and heat thoroughly, then add the boiling water. Divide in the four pans. Mix flour, sugar and butter together for the crumbs and put on top of the syrup.

Bake in moderate oven.

Brown Sugar Pie

³/₃ cupful of brown sugar
1 tablespoon butter
2 tablespoons milk
1½ teaspoons vanilla

Cook until waxy looking, then take the yolks of 2 eggs and 1 heaping tablespoon of flour and 1½ cupfuls milk. Mix all together smooth. Add to the above ingredients. Cook until thick and add vanilla. Have a baked crust, use the whites beaten stiff for the top. Return to the oven for a minute or two.

Banbury Tart

1 cup flour
2 heaping tablespoons of lard
Cold water

Handle as little as possible; roll thin and cut with cutter 6 inches in diameter.

Filling

1 egg beaten light
1 cup raisins
1 cup sugar
1 tablespoon of flour
Juice of one lemon and grated rind

Mix well and cook to consistency of custard, and fill the pastry which is turned up and made into the shape of a tart.

PUDDINGS

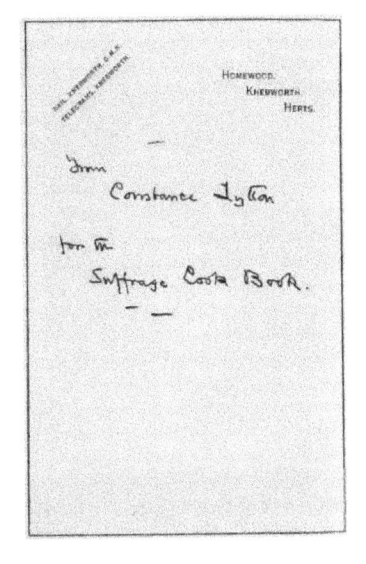

It almost makes me wish I vow to have two stomachs like a cow. Hood.

Bakewell Pudding

The famous dainty from the town of Bakewell, Derbyshire, England.

PASTE

6 oz. flour
2 oz. margarine
½ small spoon baking powder

MIXTURE

1½ ounces butter
3 ounces sugar
2 eggs
1 dessert spoon corn flour
½ cup hot water
½ small spoon lemon juice

Make the paste, roll quite thin, and line an ashet; spread bottom with jam; pour on top above mixture, prepared as follows:—melt butter, add sugar, flour, and beat well, then the water, and fruit juice; finally, the eggs, well beaten.

Bake for about ½ an hour. Serve, of course, cold.

Graham Pudding

1 cup molasses
1 cup sweet milk
1½ cups graham flour
1 egg
1 tablespoon butter
1 teaspoon cinnamon
½ teaspoon nutmeg
1 teaspoon soda
1 cup raisins

Put in buttered pudding dish and steam 3 hours.

Norwegian Prune Pudding

½ lb. prunes
2 cups cold water
1 cup sugar
1 inch piece stick cinnamon
1⅓ cups boiling water

⅓ cup corn starch
1 tablespoon lemon juice

Pick out and wash prunes; then soak 1 hour in cold water, and boil until soft; remove stones; obtain meat from stones and add to prunes; then add sugar, cinnamon, boiling water, and simmer ten minutes.

Dilute corn starch with enough cold water to pour easily; add to prune mixture and cook five minutes. Remove cinnamon; mould; then chill and serve with whipped cream.

STATE OF IDAHO
GOVERNOR'S OFFICE,
BOISE.

January 22, 1915.

Woman Suffrage has gone beyond the trial stage in Idaho. We have had it in operation for many years and it is now thoroughly and satisfactorily established. Its repeal would not carry a single county in the State.

The women form an intelligent, patriotic and energetic element in our politics. They have been instrumental in accomplishing many needed reforms along domestic and moral lines, and in creating a sentiment favorable to the strict enforcement of the law.

The impression that Woman Suffrage inspires an ambition in women to seek and hold public office is altogether wrong. The contrary is true. The women of Idaho are not politicians, but they demand faithful and conscientious service from public officials and when this service is not rendered their disapproval is certain and unmistakable.

Woman suffrage produces no wrong or injury to society, but it does engender a higher spirit of civic righteousness and places political and public affairs on a more elevated plane of morality and responsibility.

> M. ALEXANDER,
> Governor of Idaho

Suet Pudding

1 cup suet
1 cup brown sugar
1 cup raisins
1 pint flour
1 cup milk
2 teaspoons baking powder

Mix suet, chopped fine, raisins and sugar, then add flour and baking powder, add milk and steam three hours. Serve with sauce.

Plain Suet Pudding

1 cup beef suet
1 teaspoon salt
2 eggs
3½ cups flour
3 teaspoons baking powder
2 cups milk

Put suet through meat grinder or food chopper, fine blade. Sift flour, salt, baking powder and rub suet into flour well. Beat eggs lightly, add milk and stir into mixture. Butter mold and fill ¾ full and steam three hours. This quantity makes two good sized puddings.

It is very nice made without the eggs and using one-half the quantity. Fill a deep pudding dish or pan with fruit, apples or peaches, dropping the suet pudding over the fruit in large spoonsfull and steam 1½ hours.

Cottage Fruit Pudding

2 teaspoons butter
1 egg
¼ teaspoon salt
1 cup sugar

½ cup milk
1¾ cups flour

Cream well together 2 teaspoons butter, 1 cup sugar, 1 egg, ½ cup milk, ¼ teaspoon salt and 1¾ cups flour. Beat well and add two scant teaspoons baking powder, then turn into shallow, well-buttered pan, the bottom of which has been covered with fresh fruit of any kind.

Bake in moderate oven one-half hour. Serve with cream or sauce.

Prune Souffle

One-half pound of prunes, three tablespoons of powdered sugar, four eggs, a small teaspoon of vanilla. Beat the yolks of the eggs and the sugar to a cream, add the vanilla and mix them with the prunes. The prunes should first be stewed and drained, the stones removed, and each prune cut into four pieces. When ready to serve, fold in lightly the stiffly whipped whites of the eggs, having added a dash of salt to the whites before whipping.

Turn it into a pudding dish and bake in a moderate oven for 20 minutes. Serve very hot directly it is taken from the oven.

Plum Pudding

2 lbs. suet
1 lb. sugar
½ lb. flour
12 eggs
1 pint milk
2 nutmegs grated
¼ oz. cloves.
2 lbs. bread crumbs (dry)
2 lbs. raisins
2 lbs. currants
¼ lb. orange & lemon peel
1 cup brandy
½ oz. mace
¼ oz. allspice

Free suet from strings and chop fine. Seed raisins, chop fine and dredge with flour. Cream suet and sugar; beat in the yolks when whipped smooth and light; next put in milk; then flour and crumbs alternately with beaten whites; then brandy and spice, and lastly the fruit well dredged with flour. Mix all thoroughly. Take well buttered bowls filled to the top with the mixture and steam five hours. (This pudding will keep a long time).

When cold cover with cheesecloth and tie with cord around the rim of the bowl. Steam again one hour before using. Use wine or brandy sauce. When on the table pour a little brandy or rum over the top of the pudding and set fire to it. This adds much to the flavor.

Lemon Cream

Cream together the yolks of five (5) eggs and four (4) tablespoons of sugar. Add the grated rind of one (1) lemon and the juice of one and one-half (1½) lemons. Dissolve 1 teaspoon of gelatine in a very little water, while hot stir into the pudding. Let stand till it thickens, then add the beaten whites of the eggs. Serve in individual sherbet cups.

MRS. RAYMOND ROBINS.

Lemon Hard Sauce

Cream two tablespoons of butter until soft, add one tablespoon of lemon juice and a little nutmeg, then beat in enough sifted confectioner's sugar to make a light, fluffy mass. Let it harden a little before serving.

Corn Pudding

9 large ears of corn
1 tablespoon butter
1 teaspoon salt
3 eggs or 2 will do (beaten)
2 cups of boiled rice
1 cup milk
pepper and little sugar

Score and cut corn fine—scraping the last off cob. Put the butter in the hot rice. First mix rice and corn well together, then beat in the custard.

Raw Carrot Pudding

1 cup carrots, grated
1 cup potatoes, grated
1½ cups white sugar
2 cups flour
1 cup raisins
1 teaspoon soda

Salt, cinnamon, lard and nutmeg to taste. Steam three hours. Serve with whipped cream or sauce.

STATE OF ILLINOIS
GOVERNOR'S OFFICE
Springfield

Since, on viewing the past in perspective, we can derive a lesson such as is contained in the steady, sure advance of the world by successive steps toward a higher moral consciousness with a broad humanitarianism as its basis, may we not, by virtue of this fact, find the way lighted to the future—a future in which men and women will combine forces and resort to helpful co-operation in all those things which add to the sum of human happiness. If history shows that the most rapid strides toward a lofty civilization have been made since both the sexes assumed this attitude of mutual helpfulness, does it not, by that same token, reveal the source of greatest efficiency while indicating that feminism is humanism, and thus foretelling the trend of human development.

Ever yours truly,
EDWARD F. DUNNE,
Governor.

Customer—That was the driest flattest sandwich I ever tried to chew into!

Waiter—Why here's your sandwich! You ate your check.

SANDWICH RECIPES

Hawaiian Sandwiches

Chop finely one pimento, one green pepper freed from seeds, and a small cream cheese; add a good pinch of salt and spread between slices of buttered bread.

Chocolate Sandwiches

Butter and thinly slice white bread; make a chocolate filling exactly like fudge, but do not allow it to boil quite to the candy stage; spread between the slices of bread, press together and trim neatly.

Caramel Sandwiches

Melt a tablespoon of butter with a cup of light brown sugar, and a tablespoon of water; cook for a few moments, till well incorporated, then spread between slices of buttered bread.

Fruit Sandwiches

Chop candied cherries, dried figs and stoned dates together; make a paste with a little orange juice, and spread between buttered slices of graham bread.

Cucumber Sandwiches

Pare and slice cucumbers crosswise. Marinate in French dressing and place between rounds of buttered bread.

Anchovy Canapes

Cream 2 tablespoons butter; add ½ teaspoon Anchovy paste; spread thin slices of fresh toast with this; over that put slices of hard boiled or chopped egg and on top one rolled anchovy.

Sandwiches

Another delightful way of using sardines is as a sandwich. Beat two ounces of butter until it is soft, then add a little salt, nutmeg, Nepaul pepper, 2 teaspoons of tomato catsup and a few drops of lemon juice.

Remove the skin and the backbone from three sardines, and pound them to a paste in a mortar with the prepared butter.

Pass the mixture through a wire sieve and spread it rather thickly on fingershaped pieces of buttered brown bread, and make into sandwiches with a little fine cress between the bread.

Filling for Sandwiches

1 cup yellow cheese
1 cup tomato juice
½ cup chipped beef ground
1 egg beaten separately

Cook tomato juice until it thickens, add cheese, beef and egg last; if the mixture is too thick, add cream.

Apple Sandwiches

Take bran or whole wheat bread cut thin and spread thin with peanut butter. Wash, pare, quarter, core and slice the apples very thin spread between the bread. Or the bread can be buttered and thin slices of apple put between, then the apple is dusted with a little salt.

Nothing lovelier can be found in woman, than to study household good.   Milton's Paradise Lost.

SALADS AND SALAD DRESSINGS

Pear Salad

Arrange either fresh or cooked pears on lettuce leaves, and pour over pears sweet cream dressing. Over this grate cocoanut and on top place cherries.

Potato Salad

¼ Peck of very small potatoes
½ Portion Small Onion
1 Small Bunch Celery
2 Tablespoons of Sugar
4 Tablespoons Olive Oil
½ Pint of Vinegar
Salt and Pepper to taste

Boil potatoes until soft; pare and let cool, then slice very thin; add finely cut onions and diluted vinegar enough to mix well; add salt, pepper and sugar, some celery cut fine and lastly olive oil.

Serenely full, the epicure would say Fate cannot harm me, I have dined today.   Sidney Smith

Codfish Salad

1 piece of codfish
½ cup diluted vinegar
black pepper to season
1 cup cold boiled potatoes, slices very thin
1 tablespoon chopped parsley
1 hard boiled egg
1 teaspoon olive oil

Soak fish over night. Place in fresh water and bring to the boiling point. Do not allow it to boil. Take out fish and shred. Remove all skin and bones. Allow it to cool.

Add potatoes, parsley, pepper, oil and vinegar.

Swedish Wreathes

Work 1 cup of bread dough, ¼ cup butter and ¼ cup lard, using the hands. When thoroughly blended, toss on floured board and knead, using enough flour to prevent sticking.

Cut off pieces and roll like bread stick; shape into rings, dip upper surface in blanched almonds that have been chopped and salted. Arrange on buttered baking sheets.

Bake in hot oven until brown.

Bean Salad

¼ peck Green String Beans
½ small onion
½ cup vinegar
½ cup sweet or sour cream
2 tablespoons sugar
½ tablespoon salt
⅛ teaspoon pepper or paprika

Boil the beans until tender in salt water, not soft, drain and let cool. When cold add the onion, cut fine; mix the cream, vinegar, salt, sugar and pepper and pour over beans; serve very cold on lettuce leaves.

Hard boiled eggs can be used as a garnish.

Mrs. F. M. Roessing.

Hot Slaw

1 small head cabbage
1 onion
1 tablespoon bacon fat
1 teaspoon sugar
1 teaspoon vinegar
salt to taste

Cut cabbage not too fine, heat fat in sauce pan. Wash cabbage and put into that a little water and add onion, cut up, salt and a little pepper. Cook about twenty minutes, then add the sugar and vinegar.

It must be sour-sweet. It is then ready to serve.

Creole Salad

Cut off the tops of eight medium sized sweet bell peppers, saving the tops with the stems attached; remove all the seeds and white portion without breaking the pepper, then throw them into ice water for 30 minutes.

Mix together a cupful of minced ham and chicken, four hard boiled eggs and a bunch of celery, chopped, and a Spanish Onion.

Moisten with dressing, fill the shells, replace the tops and serve.

COLORED SALADS

A Salad to Fit in With Any Scheme of Decoration You May Wish to Carry Out.

Yellow

To make a yellow salad use the yellower heart leaves of lettuce. On them put diced orange pulp, dressed with French dressing and sprinkled with chopped walnut meats. Or else scoop out the centers of small yellow-skinned apples and fill them with a mixture of orange and apple, dressed with mayonnaise made with lemon juice for thinning and a flavoring of mustard.

Green

On green, but tender leaves of lettuce, put a little mound of spinach, which has been boiled and pressed through a sieve and mixed with French dressing. In the center of each mound, concealed by the spinach, put a spoonful of chopped hard-boiled egg.

Green and White

Peel and boil tiny white turnips of equal size and hollow out the center of each. Fill with cold boiled peas and mayonnaise and put on green lettuce leaves.

White

Celery, potato, chicken—white meat only—white fish, blanched asparagus—any or two of these may be used for white salad. Dress with French dressing or with a white mayonnaise, to which the beaten white of egg has been added and which has been thinned with vinegar.

Red

Scoop out the inside of tomatoes. Save the slice removed from the top for a cover and replace it on the tomato after filling it with a mixture of celery and nut meats, mixed with mayonnaise. Place each tomato on a white leaf of lettuce.

Pink

Strain tomato juice and mix it with equal quantity of white stock—veal or chicken. Thicken sufficiently with gelatin and harden in molds. Serve on white lettuce leaves, with mayonnaise that has been colored with a little cranberry juice.

Orange Salad

Make mayonnaise with much egg yolk in proportion to other ingredients, and thin with cider vinegar. Dice tender carrots and arrange on lettuce leaves, dressing with orange mayonnaise.

> Animals feed, Men eat, but only intelligent Men know what to eat.   Brillat Savarin

Tomato Aspic

In Tomato Aspic—Tomato jellies with sardines should be made in ample time to harden on ice. The aspic referred to is ordinary gelatin mixed with soup stock instead of plain water. Remove the skin from sardines, then split them open and take out the backbone and cut them into narrow strips.

Mix together in equal quantities some stiff mayonnaise sauce and cool, but liquid, aspic jelly then stir in some chopped capers and small pieces of tomato, in the proportion of a dessertspoon of each to half a pint of the mayonnaise and aspic mixture; and, lastly, add the sardines.

Have at hand some small tomato molds which have been rather thickly lined with tomato aspic, fill them with the sardine mixture and leave on ice until the jellies can be unmolded; serve each on a small leaf of lettuce, and surround with a salad of water-cress and sliced tomatoes.

Suffrage Salad Dressing

Yolks of 2 eggs
3 tablespoons of sugar
2 tablespoons of tarragon vinegar
1 pinch of salt

Beat well; cook in double boiler. When cold and ready to serve, fold in ½ pint of whipped cream.

Cucumber Aspic

Four large cucumbers, one small onion, half a box of gelatine soaked in half a cup of cold water, salt and white pepper to taste. Peel the cucumbers, cut into thick slices and place, with the sliced onion, over the fire with a scant quart of water. Simmer for an hour, stir in the gelatine and, when this is dissolved, season the jelly, strain it and set aside to cool. It may be formed into small moulds and turned out on lettuce leaves, or used in a border-mould for garnishing a fish or tomato salad, or set to form in a salad bowl and taken out by the spoonful and served on lettuce leaves. French dressing is better with it than mayonnaise.

Boiled Mayonnaise Dressing

1 egg
1 piece of butter size of walnut
1 tablespoon of sugar
½ teaspoon of mustard
½ teaspoon of salt
½ teaspoon white pepper
1 tablespoon cider vinegar
1 tablespoon boiling water just before putting in double boiler.

Mix dry ingredients and beaten egg. Add melted butter and vinegar. Beat well until thoroughly mixed. Add boiling water; cook until thick. Use level measures. If too thick use plain cream to thin.

Mayonnaise Dressing Without Oil

2 Table spoons Dry Mustard
2   "   "   Salt
2   "   "   Flour
2   "   "   Sugar

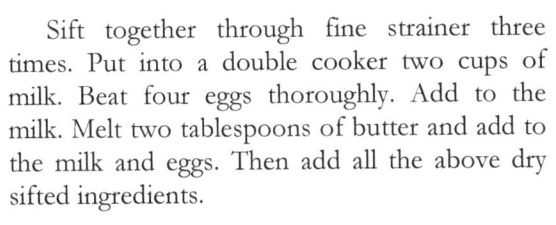

Sift together through fine strainer three times. Put into a double cooker two cups of milk. Beat four eggs thoroughly. Add to the milk. Melt two tablespoons of butter and add to the milk and eggs. Then add all the above dry sifted ingredients.

Put on fire, stirring constantly. When it begins to thicken add drop by drop one-half teacup vinegar.

Cook until thick, which will be about twenty minutes.

Remove from fire and put in cool place.

Mrs. Oliver H. P. Belmont,
President Political Equality Ass'n.
New York.

French Dressing

½ teaspoon salt
2 tablespoons lemon juice
½ teaspoon pepper
4 tablespoons olive oil

Alabama Dressing

2 cups of oil
yolks of 3 eggs
½ cup of vinegar

Make this carefully into a smooth and well blended mayonnaise. It will take fully ½ hour, but the success of the dressing depends upon the mayonnaise. Now stir in slowly ½ bottle chili sauce until well mixed with the mayonnaise. Then chop together very fine 1 bunch of chives, 3 hard boiled eggs, 2 pimentos, ½ green pepper; add paprika and salt to taste and mix well with the mayonnaise.

This will make about 1 quart of dressing. It should be kept in a cool place and covered when not in use. It will keep a long time.

Cooked Salad Dressing

Yolks 2 eggs
½ teaspoon dry mustard
½ teaspoon salt
4 tablespoons butter
6 tablespoons hot vinegar
1 tablespoon sugar

Beat yolks until creamy, add to them the mustard, salt and sugar. Beat in slowly the butter melted, also add vinegar. Cook until it thickens. It is best to make this in a double boiler. When cold, add 1 cup sweet or sour cream.

This keeps well and is particularly fine for lettuce, celery, beans, asparagus or cauliflower.

Caviare Dressing

(For Tomato Salad)

2 heaping tablespoons of caviare
Yolks of 2 eggs, boiled hard and grated
One tablespoon of chopped onions
¼ tablespoon of paprika
4 tablespoons of olive oil
2 tablespoons of tarragon vinegar

MEAT AND FISH SAUCES

Bechamel Sauce

1½ cups whitestock
1 slice onion
1 slice carrot
Bit of Bay leaf
Sprig of parsley
⅛ teaspoon pepper
6 peppercorns
¼ cup butter
¼ cup flour
1 cup scalded milk
½ teaspoon salt

Cook white stock 20 minutes with onion, carrot, bay leaf, parsley and peppercorns, and then strain; there should be one cupful.

Melt the butter, add flour, and gradually the hot stock and milk. Season with salt and pepper.

A Sauce for Hot Meats

½ cup sharp vinegar
2 tablespoons Colman's Mustard
a little Tabasco Sauce
2 tablespoons Horse Radish
½ cup butter melted very hot
Pepper and salt to taste

A warmed-up dinner was never worth much

—Boileau.

Gravy Warmed Over for Meats

One-half cup walnut catsup, 1 wine glass tomato catsup, 1 small cup sherry (may be omitted), 1 tablespoon butter, rubbed smooth with flour, 1 small onion chopped very fine, 1 teaspoon currant jelly, salt and pepper.

When thoroughly mixed lay slices of the meat in a dish, pour the gravy over, then set dish in the oven until all is well heated through. Serve.

Horse Radish Sauce

Make a plain white sauce and season to taste. When done add ¾ cup of grated horseradish and ½ cup cream.

Very good for meats, especially boiling meat.

STATE OF KANSAS.

Jan. 6, 1914.

Editress Suffrage Cook Book:

What do I think of woman suffrage? I wrote the resolution in the Kansas Senate submitting the constitutional amendment for it. When I became Governor of Kansas I found a hundred little orphans at our State Orphans' Home, mothered by a man. The little unfortunates at our schools for the deaf and the blind were mothered by men. I placed women at the head of these institutions. Among the other appointees during my term of office was a woman on the Board of Administration, the board having our educational institutions in charge; a woman on the Board of Health; a woman Factory Inspector; a woman Parole Officer; a woman on the State Text Book Commission; two women on the Board of Education, and women physicians at our state hospitals. In every instance these women gave the State of Kansas better service than did the men whom they succeeded.

The women of Kansas have "arrived" and the state service is better by their participating in it.

Cordially yours,
GEORGE H. HODGES.
Governor.

Cooking takes a little training and a great deal of common sense.

EGGS, ETC.

Pain d'Oeufs

Beat slightly six eggs, add six tablespoons sugar, a pinch of salt and one-half teaspoon vanilla. Scald three cups of milk and pour slowly over the eggs, stirring constantly.

Melt in a granite or aluminum baking dish six tablespoons of sugar until brown, using no water. Pour the custard into this, set into a pan of hot water and bake in a slow oven 45 minutes or more until the custard is set, and a testing knife comes out clean. The water in the pan must not boil.

When perfectly cold turn upside down into a glass or china serving dish.

MRS. CARRIE CHAPMAN CATT.

Bread Crumb Omelet

4 eggs
small teaspoon salt
little minced onion
4 or 5 cups bread crumbs
2 cups milk
4 sprigs parsley (minced fine)
minced sweet green peppers can be added
¼ cup butter softened (melt and cool)

Beat all well together, pour into a buttered dish and bake in a slow oven until lightly browned.

Should be served at once, as it sinks down when cooling. This does not harm it only it does not look so pretty. If it browns too quickly—cover.

Egg Patties

Beat eggs lightly and add crushed cracker crumbs till it forms a thick paste, then thin with a little milk. Season with finely cut onion, pepper and salt. Fry in butter, like pancakes. Very good and something different.

God sends meat and the devil sends cooks.

John Taylor

Florentine Eggs in Casseroles

Chop cooked spinach very fine and season with butter and salt. Put 1 tablespoon spinach in each buttered individual casserole, sprinkle with 1 teaspoon grated Parmesan cheese, and slip into each an egg. Cover each egg with ½ teaspoon grated Parmesan cheese and 1 teaspoon Bechamel sauce.

Bake until the eggs are set, and serve immediately. This makes a delicious entree.

Cheese Souffle

3 eggs beaten separately very light
1 cup sour cream
1 cup grated cheese
2 teaspoons finely sifted flour

Bake in a quick oven in buttered baking dish.

Oyster Omelet

½ pint oysters
3 eggs
salt and pepper to taste
2½ tablespoons butter

Drain oysters. Put butter in pan and cook oysters until they curl. Beat eggs lightly and put over oysters; season and shake until done. Serve at once.

Potato Omelet

3 medium potatoes
1 large spoon butter
½ tablespoon lard
5 eggs

½ onion minced
season to taste

Scrape the potatoes into cold water to keep from discoloring. Put butter and lard in skillet, and brown carefully, add potato squeezed out of the water also onion, cook slowly and then beat the eggs and add.

When done on one side put a plate over the skillet and turn the omelet, now slip in the pan and brown the other side. Serve at once.

"Well, Marie" said Jiggles after the town election "for whom did you vote this morning?"

"I crossed off the names of all the candidates," returned Mrs. Jiggles, "and wrote out my principles on the back of my ballot. This is no time to consider individuals and their little personal ambitions."—New York Times.

Northampton, Mass.
Dec. 22, 1914.

Editress Suffrage Cook Book:

As to a sentiment on equal suffrage, let me say that if I had no more generous reason for approving it, I should do so on the ground of my opposition to seeing any element of our people enjoying large liberty and influence without the restraints of a corresponding responsibility in the suffrage.

Ever yours truly,
G. W. CABLE.

CREAMS, CUSTARDS, ETC.

Strawberry Short Cake a la Mode

>1 cup flour
>½ teaspoon Baking powder
>¼ teaspoon salt
>1 heaping tablespoon of butter

Sift the dry ingredients together and work in the butter. Mix with enough milk to make a stiff dough which can be rolled as thin as a wafer.

Put one thin layer on a pie-pan and butter lightly; lay another layer on first. Bake eight minutes in a moderate oven.

When cold cut in pieces and split each piece. Place a large tablespoon of crushed, sweetened strawberries between the layers, add the top layer, add more berries, and last of all, a heaping tablespoon of ice cream or frozen custard.

Frozen Custard

(for above Short Cake)

To 1 pint of milk add ½ pint of cream. Scald. Have ready 1 egg, well beaten, 1 scant cup of granulated sugar, and one level tablespoon of cornstarch.

Add this mixture to the milk and cream as soon as they come to a boil. Stir and set aside to cool. When cold, add 1 teaspoon of vanilla and freeze.

Stewed Apples

Cut apples in quarters and immediately put in saucepan and pour over them boiling water just to cover.

Put on lid and boil quickly until tender. Sprinkle sugar over them to taste. But never stir the apples at any time. When sugar is on leave the lid off, let cook about five minutes longer, never stirring.

Ready to serve, hot or cold.

Cinnamon Apples

>3 cups sugar—pinch salt
>2½ cups water
>1 cup cinnamon drops

8 apples

Make a syrup of water and sugar. Put in cinnamon drops. Pare and core apples. Place in syrup and boil until tender, do not allow to break.

Take out when tender and place in a dish or if you wish in individual dishes. Pour over syrup, and allow to cool. When cold pour whipped cream on top of each and a cherry on top of cream.

Fire Apples

Select bright red apples, cut off the tops and with a knife remove the meat, leaving only sufficient wall to hold apple in shape. Make a filling of the following:

To six apples allow about twelve tablespoons of very dry cooked rice, six tablespoons cracker crumbs, six tablespoons chopped apples, six tablespoons sugar, six tablespoons seeded raisins, six tablespoons chopped almonds.

Whip one egg thoroughly, place in a cup and fill the cup with milk; stir well and place in a double boiler, adding one-half teaspoon butter, grated rind and juice of one-half lemon and a dash of nutmeg. Cook until it thickens, cool, then mix it into the filling, being careful not to get it too soft. Mold lightly with the fingers and fill the apples, sprinkle with sugar, add a cupful of water and bake in a moderate oven. Serve with whipped cream or custard sauce.

Candied Cranberry Recipe

> 1 quart berries
> 2 cups sugar
> 1½ large cups of hot or cold water
> pinch of soda

Wash and make a little slit in each berry. For each quart of berries put one and a half large cups of hot or cold water in kettle. Then the berries, then spread 2 cups sugar over them, also a pinch of soda. Keep covered closely all the time, do not stir or lift lid until perfectly cold. From the moment it begins to boil count five minutes—no more—to cook them.

If you remove the lid the lovely gloss will be lost.

Apple Rice

1 cup of rice boiled in water with a piece of butter and a little salt until half done. Then add six apples cut in pieces. Cook together until both rice and apples are well done. Add sugar to taste. When ready to serve pour over melted butter browned. Serve with sugar and cinnamon.

Jelly Whip

Dissolve one package of gelatin in a cupful of cold water. Add to that two cupfuls of sugar and one quart of boiling water. Divide the mixture into three parts, in one of which place marshmallows and white grapes. In the second one put pineapple and oranges and in the third nuts. Fill individual glasses with different mixtures and serve them with whipped cream. Decorate with preserved cherries, candied orange peel and nuts.

Pineapple Parfait

Pare and shred a ripe pineapple, add one cup of sugar and let stand for several hours. Drain off one cup of the juice, boil it with three-quarters of a cup of sugar for 10 minutes. Add slowly to well beaten yolks of four eggs, and cook in a double boiler, stirring all the time, until the mixture will coat the spoon. Remove from the fire and beat until cold. Then add two tablespoons of lemon juice and two cups of cream whipped to a stiff froth.

Pack in a mold, cover tightly and surround with ice and salt for four hours.

Rice

3/4 cup of rice washed 7 times
1/2 cup currants
1 1/4 cups milk
Yolk of 1 egg
2 1/2 tablespoons sugar
1 small piece lemon rind

Boil rice in a large quantity of boiling water for 20 minutes; drain and add milk, sugar, lemon rind, currants. Let cook slowly for 15 minutes and remove from fire; beat the yolk of an egg in a little milk and stir in the rice.

Do not set back on the fire. Serve cold.

Pittsburgh Sherbet

Take a cupful of the syrup from a jar of raspberry preserves and the same amount of juice from a can of pineapple; add two tablespoons of lemon juice and a syrup made by boiling together a pint of water and a cupful of sugar. When cold add four tablespoons of orange juice and freeze. When stiff, open the freezer and add the white of an egg, beaten stiff with a teaspoon of powdered sugar.

Lemon Sherbet

1 quart milk
2 cups sugar
juice 3 lemons

Dissolve sugar in milk, place in freezer. Add lemon juice after freezer has been packed. Add juice rapidly and with violent stirring, then immediately place in dasher and turn the crank until frozen.

Fruit Cocktails

Peel and cut one orange and one grapefruit into small pieces, removing all seeds and white bits of skin, add two sliced bananas, a tablespoon of chopped or grated pineapple, sweeten to taste, and mix with the juice from a can of pineapple. Stand in a very cold place, or put in the ice cream freezer and partially freeze, serve in small glasses and ornament with maraschino cherries. Reserve the remaining pineapple for a luncheon dish.

Synthetic Quince

An Accidental Discovery

I put too much water with my rhubarb and had a whole dishful of beautiful pink juice left over, about a quart. In this I cooked some apples, quartered, and stewed till soft, and just as an experiment added a saucerful of strawberries—also "left over."

The result, being served, looked and tasted exactly like quince, except that the apple was a little softer.

CHARLOTTE PERKIN GILMAN.

Grape Juice Cup

Soak the grated rind of one orange in the juice of one lemon for 15 minutes. To this add a cupful of boiling water and a tablespoon of sugar.

Place in a saucepan of granite ware and add one quart of unfermented grape juice, four whole cloves and a pinch of powdered mace. Bring slowly to the boiling point and simmer for ten minutes.

Boil together one cupful of sugar and two tablespoons of water without stirring until it spins a thread.

Pour this gradually upon the stiffly beaten whites of two eggs. Add the boiling grape juice, dust lightly with grated nutmeg and serve immediately.

Live while you live, the epicure would say and seize the pleasures of the present day.   Doddridge

Peppermint Cup

Soak half an ounce of pulverized gum arabic in half a cupful of cold water for 30 minutes. Dissolve it over hot water.

Add one cupful of powdered sugar and cook until it will spin a thread.

Pour this upon the stiffly beaten whites of two eggs, and when well blended add gradually a pint of boiling cream, a few drops of essence of peppermint and a tiny pinch of baking soda.

Serve while it foams, sprinkled with a little powdered cinnamon.

Unquiet meals make ill digestions.

Comedy of Errors

Amber Marmalade

1 orange
1 grape fruit
1 lemon

Slice very thin. Measure the fruit and add 3 times the quantity of water. Stand in an earthen dish over night and in morning boil for ten minutes. Stand another night and the second morning add pint for pint of sugar and boil steadily until it jellies.

This should make 8 or 10 glasses but the size of fruit determines the quantity. Stir as little as possible during the two hours or more of the cooking which it requires. Do not use the rind of the grape fruit.

Grape Juice

5 lbs Concord Grapes
1 quart water
sugar

Boil grapes five to ten minutes. Then strain through a wire strainer and afterwards cheese cloth. To every quart of juice add 1 lb. sugar. Bottle and seal.

PRESERVES, PICKLES, ETC.

Sour Pickles

1 peck green tomatoes
1 lb. figs
1 lb. seeded raisins
1 cup vinegar
4 cups sugar
20 cloves
A few sticks cinnamon

Sweet Pickles

Tomato and Fig Pickles

One peck of green tomatoes sliced and salted in layers, place in granite boiler over night. In the morning drain off brine and rinse in cold water.

Chop up a pound of figs, add to the tomatoes, cover with vinegar and boil twenty minutes; add 1 pound of seeded raisins, 1 cup of vinegar, 4 cups of sugar, 20 cloves and a few sticks of cinnamon tied in a cheese cloth bag, and cook together slowly for ¾ of an hour.

LUCRETIA L. BLANKENBURG.

Lemon Butter

6 eggs
3 very large lemons (rind and juice)
2 cups sugar
2 tablespoons water
butter size of walnut

Mix all together with Dove egg beater and cook until it boils. Watch that it does not burn.

Kumquat Preserves

1 quart fruit to 1 pint sugar

Cut the Kumquats into halves, pick out seeds, cover with cold water and bring to a boil. In the meantime have your syrup boiling—1 pint sugar to 3 pints water.

Drain fruit and put in syrup and simmer slowly for 1 hour. Take out fruit and continue to simmer syrup until it begins to get thick.

Put the fruit into syrup—place preserving kettle in pot of boiling water and let them, or let the water continue boiling until syrup is thick as you like it. Put ¼ teaspoon fine salt in first water, as it adds a fine flavor. Grate stem off skin deep.

STATE OF WASHINGTON
OFFICE OF GOVERNOR
OLYMPIA.

December 22, 1914.

Editress Suffrage Cook Book:

I have at hand your letter of the 16th inst., asking an expression from me regarding Woman Suffrage in the State of Washington.

Replying, I desire to say that the women of the State of Washington have had the right to vote for something more than three years. I know of no one who was in favor of giving them this right who to-day opposes it, and large numbers of those who were opposed now favor women having the ballot. The results in the State of Washington certainly indicate that women assist in public affairs, rather than otherwise, by having the right to vote.

Agreeable to your request, I am sending a photograph of myself under separate cover; also card carrying my autograph.

Yours very truly,
ERNEST LISTER,
Governor.

Hire me twenty cooks.

—Shakespeare

Prunes and Chestnuts

3 lbs. dried prunes
2 lbs. large chestnuts
½ lb. Sultana raisins
1 table spoon butter
½ cup of sugar
⅓ cup of vinegar
Pinch of cloves
2 tea spoons of flour

Peel chestnuts and boil until skin can be removed. Boil prunes and raisins together until soft, add chestnuts, sugar, salt, cloves and butter, when well cooked thicken with flour and vinegar stirred together.

Heavenly Hash

2 boxes red raspberries
2 quarts red currants
2 quarts cherries
1 quart gooseberries

Stem currants and seed cherries, then measure fruit. To each cup of fruit allow equal amount of sugar. Put the fruit in kettle and add ½ cup of water; when it comes to boil add sugar and boil 20 minutes, then put in jelly glasses.

Apple Butter

1 peck tart apples (made into sauce and strained)
1 quart grape juice
2 teaspoons cinnamon
½ teaspoon salt
2 cups light brown sugar
2 teaspoons nutmeg

Boil two hours or longer.

Orange Marmalade

6 oranges
2 lemons

Slice in small pieces, add six pints of water and let stand in covered dish for 24 hours. Then boil 1¼ hours; let stand another 24 hours. Then add pint for pint of sugar with the mixture and boil until it jells. (About 45 minutes).

Rhubarb and Fig Jam

Cut five pounds rhubarb into inch pieces without peeling. Add one pound figs, four pounds sugar, the grated yellow rind and juice of one lemon and let stand all night. In the morning simmer for an hour. Nut meats may be added if desired.

Brandied Peaches

Take off skins with boiling water. For each pound of fruit allow ½ cupful of sugar and ½ pint of water. When syrup is boiling, put in peaches, a few at a time, and cook until done, but not too soft. Just pierce with straw.

Spread on platters to cool.

When cool, put in jars and fill up with the syrup mixed with just as much good brandy.

Have syrup thick and seal hot.

Cauliflower Pickles

3 heads cauliflower
2 quarts cucumbers cut in cubes
1 quart onions cut fine
1 pint green peppers cut fine

Mustard Sauce

1 quart vinegar (if white wine vinegar use 1 pint water and 1 pint vinegar as it is too strong)
6 tablespoons mustard (Coleman's)
1 teaspoon tumeric
1 cup (small) flour
2 cups sugar
3 tablespoons salt

Boil onions, peppers in the vinegar; then add the cucumber. After it has boiled a few minutes add the cauliflower and then the mustard sauce. Boil together a few minutes; bottle and seal hot.

The cauliflower must be boiled alone before adding.

This is very excellent.

Relish

30 large tomatoes
8 large onions
8 large red peppers
5 tablespoons salt
10 tablespoons sugar
9 cups vinegar

Cut the tomatoes and onions and boil one hour with the sugar, vinegar and salt; at the end of an hour put it through a sieve; now return to the stove and add your red peppers, cut very fine, and cook one more hour. Have it about the consistency of thick cream and bottle hot. Very fine for cold meats, fish, etc.

Chili Sauce

30 large red tomatoes
12 medium sized onions
4 red peppers
3 teaspoons salt
12 teaspoons brown sugar
10 cups cider vinegar

Chop tomatoes by themselves, then add finely chopped onions and peppers. Lastly add sugar, salt and vinegar mixing well. Boil 2 hours and can.

Pickles

1 peck medium sized pickles
1 gallon cider vinegar
1 cup sugar
1 cup mustard
1 cup salt

Wash pickles well and pack in stone crock. Dissolve mustard in some of the vinegar and mix all together and pour over pickles cold. Put on a weight—ready to use in three days.

Tomato Pickle

2 gallon crocks of sliced green tomatoes sprinkled with salt.
4 small sliced onions mixed and let stand
2 quarts cider vinegar, heated and added
5 cents' worth mixed spices
2 lbs. brown sugar, and boil.

Makes 3 quarts of pickles Corn Salad

2 doz. ears of corn; boil twenty minutes on cob. Cut off cob; chop one head cabbage; 3 green peppers, and 1 red pepper. Mix together. Put in kettle with four pints vinegar; 3 tablespoons salt, 2 tablespoons ground mustard; 4 cups sugar; 2 teaspoons celery seed. Cook 20 minutes.

Tomato Catsup (very fine)

To ½ bushel skinned Tomatoes, add
1 quart good vinegar
1 pound salt
1 pound black pepper (whole)
1 ounce African Cayenne pepper
¼ pound allspice (whole)
1 ounce cloves
3 small boxes mustard (use less if you do not wish it very hot)
4 cloves of garlic
6 onions (large)
1 pound brown sugar
1 pint peach leaves

Boil this mass for 3 hours, stirring constantly to keep from burning. When cool, strain through a sieve and bottle for use. Vegetable coloring may be used if you wish it to remain a bright red. (A family recipe handed down for generations and very good, indeed).

CANDIES, ETC.

Five Oz. Childhood Fondant

    1 oz. kindness
    1 oz. sunshine
    1 oz. pure food
    1 oz. recreation
    1 oz. rest

This should be on hand in every household where children gladden the hearth. Wherever possible distribute it among the little children of the poor.

Rose Leaves Candied

Take red roses, remove all the whites at the bottom. Take three times their weight in sugar, put a pint of water to a pint of roses, skin well, shred the roses a little before you put them into the water, and cover them, and when the leaves are tender, put in the sugar.

Keep stirring lest they burn and the syrup be consumed.

Delicious Fudge

Delicious fudge is made with sour cream instead of fresh milk or cream.

Taffy

    2 lbs. brown sugar
    1 tablespoon butter
    1 tablespoon golden syrup
    ¾ cup water
    1 teaspoon vanilla
    1 tablespoon white vinegar

Mix well and allow it to boil slowly. Skim but do not stir. Boil until a little hardens in water. Then add the vanilla and vinegar.

Now pour into buttered tins and when the edges harden, draw lightly to the center. When cool pull until light. When doing so flour the hands lightly.

Creole Balls

Chop half a cupful each of almonds, pecans and walnuts and add enough fondant to make the mixture of the right consistency to mold into bonbons. Boil into little balls and dip in maple or chocolate fondant.

Chocolate Caramels

1 pint brown sugar
1 gill milk
½ pint molasses
½ cake sweetened chocolate
1 generous teaspoon butter
1 tablespoon vanilla

Boil all of the ingredients (except the vanilla) over a slow fire until dissolved, and stir occasionally as it burns easily. Test by dropping little in water. If it hardens quickly, remove at once from the fire. Add vanilla and pour into buttered pans.

When cool, cut in squares with a buttered knife.

Sea Foam

For sea foam candy cook three cupfuls of light brown sugar, a cupful of water and a tablespoon of vinegar until the syrup forms a hard ball when dropped into cold water. Pour it slowly over the stiffly beaten whites of two eggs, beating continually until the candy is stiff enough to hold its shape. Then work in half a cupful of chopped nuts and half a teaspoon of vanilla. Drop in small pieces on waxed paper.

How to Make Good Coffee

When the National Coffee Roasters' Association tells how to make good coffee the housewife is naturally interested, no matter how fervently the family may praise her own brew. Coffee is the business of these gentlemen. They know it from the scientific standpoint as well as practically. Their opinion as to the best method of preparing it for the table is, therefore, worth consideration.

They tell us, first of all, that the virtues of the infusion depend primarily upon the fineness with which the roasted bean is ground. Careful experiments have shown, indeed, that when pulverized it gives a larger yield of full strength beverage than in any other shape, so that such grinding is urged in the interest of economy, as well as from a gastronomic standpoint.

The grinding, however, must be done immediately before the coffee is made. Otherwise no little of the delicate and much prized flavor of the bean will escape.

The method of making the infusion is governed by the solubility of the various elements composing the coffee. The caffeine and caffetannic acid readily dissolve in cold water, but the delicate flavoring oils require a considerable degree of heat. It so happens that water at the boiling point,

212 deg. F., is twice as effective in extracting these flavors as when at a temperature of 150 deg. F.

Nevertheless, the usual method of boiling the coffee is unsparingly condemned by the association. The infusion thus made is very high in caffeine and tannic acid. It is muddy, too, and overrich in dissolved fibrous and bitter matters. As most of the deleterious effects of coffee are due to dissolved tannin, owing to excessive boiling or the use of grounds a second time, this method of making the beverage is unqualifiedly condemned.

Steeping—that is, placing the coffee in cold water and permitting it to come to a boil—is also deprecated. An infusion so made contains less caffeine, to be sure, but it lacks the desired aromatic flavor and the characteristic coffee taste.

In fine, the association leans to a method of coffee making known as filtration. This consists in pouring boiling water once through finely pulverized coffee confined in a close-meshed muslin bag. The resultant infusion is one in which the percentage of tannin is extremely low. There is a medium amount of caffeine, but the full flavor and characteristic taste are present.

STATE OF OREGON
EXECUTIVE DEPARTMENT
SALEM.

Dec. 22, 1914.

Editress Suffrage Cook Book:

This is to acknowledge yours of the 16th instant, in reference to women's suffrage, and in reply will say that while this right has been enjoyed but a short time by our women, they have been making excellent use of it. They are prompt to register and vote, and their influence is most always found upon the side of better government. The result of their efforts is already being reflected in a number of important measures recently adopted in this state, which will make for the public good.

Very truly yours,
OSWALD WEST.
Governor.

Cottage Cheese

To make cottage cheese effectively, with an aroma and delicacy equal to its nourishment, a rich milk which has not lost time in souring should be put in an earthenware or stone jar with the lid on, and placed in hot water over a very slow fire until it is well heated with the curd clotted from the whey. When it begins to steam the curd is drained a very short period through cheese cloth. Well mixed with salt and butter and pepper it is an ideal muscle and tissue maker.

Cottage cheese is much more easily turned into brawn, brain and bone than any of the less porous, less ripe cheeses. In fact the curious uncomfortably bloated sensation experienced by many who eat other varieties of cheese is uncommon with cottage cheese.

Faulty mastication, peculiar susceptibilities to casein and an excess of other solid foods often causes the distress which follows cheese eating. If well emulsified with saliva by the teeth or mixed with water and not gulped down, cottage cheese serves every sort of food purpose.

ALBUMINOUS BEVERAGES

The following recipes were kindly contributed by Alida Frances Pattee, author of "Practical Dietetics," an invaluable book for the home.

When a large amount of nutriment is required the albuminized drinks are valuable.

The egg is a fluid food until its albumen is coagulated by heat. Often the white of egg, dissolved in water or milk, and flavored, is given when the yolk cannot be digested, as 30 per cent. of the yolk is fat. Egg-nog is very nutritious, and is extensively prescribed in certain non-febrile diseases, especially for the forced alimentation of phthisis and melancholia. There are occasional cases of bilious habit, in which eggs to be digested must be beaten in wine. But the combination of egg, milk and sugar with alcohol, which constitutes egg-nog, is apt to produce nausea and vomiting in a feeble stomach, especially in fever. For this reason whole eggs are unfit for fever patients, and the whites only should be used.

Albuminized drinks are most easily prepared cold. When a hot liquid is used, it must be poured very slowly into the well-beaten egg, stirring constantly, so that lumps of coagulated albumen do not form.

For the Diabetic. In all the albuminous drinks substitute Sweetina for the sugar. The fuel value will be 60 calories less in every recipe than when one tablespoon of sugar is used.

Energy Value of an Egg

1 medium egg (without shell) 60 Calories
1 white of egg (average) 13 "
1 yolk of egg (average) 48 "

Egg Broth, 319 Calories[1]

Yolk 1 egg
1 tablespoon sugar
Speck salt
1 cup hot milk
Brandy or some other stimulant if required.

Beat egg, add sugar and salt. Pour on carefully the hot milk. Flavor as desired, if with brandy or wine, use about one tablespoon.

NOTE.—Dried and rolled bread crumbs may be added, if desired. The whole egg may be used. Hot water, broth or coffee, may be substituted for the milk; nutmeg may be substituted for the stimulant.

Egg-Nog No. I, 231 Calories[2]

1 egg
Speck salt
¾ tablespoon sugar
¾ Cup milk
1½ tablespoon wine or
1 tablespoon brandy (or less)

Beat the egg, add the sugar and salt; blend thoroughly, add the milk and liquor. Serve immediately.

NOTE.—Have eggs and milk chilled before blending. A grating of nutmeg may be substituted for the stimulant. A lemonade shaker may be used for the blending.

Egg-Nog No. II, 231 Calories[2]

1 egg
¾ tablespoon sugar
Speck salt
¾ Cup milk
1 tablespoon brandy (or less)

Separate egg. Beat yolk, add sugar and salt, and beat until creamy. Add the milk and brandy. Beat the white till foamy (not stiff and dry), and fold it in lightly. Serve immediately.

Junket Egg-Nog, 289 Calories[3]

1 egg
1 cup milk
1 tablespoon sugar
2 teaspoons rum, brandy or wine
½ Hansen's Junket Tablet

Beat white and yolk of egg separately, very light; blend the two. Add the sugar dissolved in the rum. Heat the milk luke warm, stir into the egg mixture, and add quickly the tablet dissolved in cold water. Pour into small warm glasses, and sprinkle grated nutmeg over the top. Stand in warm room undisturbed until firm, and then put on ice to cool. This can be retained by the most delicate stomach.

Beef Egg-Nog, 200 Calories

1 egg
Speck salt
1 tablespoon sugar
½ cup hot beef broth
1 tablespoon brandy

Beat the egg slightly, add the salt and sugar; add gradually the hot broth; add brandy and strain. Sugar and brandy may be omitted if preferred.

Coffee Egg-Nog, 175 Calories[4]

1 egg
1½ teaspoon sugar
½ scant cup milk or cream
½ scant cup strong coffee

Chill ingredients, and blend as for Egg-nog No. II.

Pineapple Egg-Nog

Prepare as per Egg-nog No I or II; omit the brandy and use pineapple juice to taste.

Egg and Rum, 315 Calories

1 cup fresh milk
Yolk 1 egg
1 tablespoon sugar
Speck salt
Few grains nutmeg
1 tablespoon rum

Beat yolk, add sugar, salt and nutmeg; add milk and rum.

NOTE.—For consumptives, taken at about 6 A. M., often prevents the exhaustive sweats which accompany the morning doze. Also may be given to a patient before dressing to prevent exhaustion.

Egg and Brandy, 350 Calories[5]

3 Eggs
4 tablespoons cold water
Nutmeg
4 tablespoons brandy

Sugar

Beat the eggs, add cold water, brandy and sweeten to taste. A little nutmeg may be added. Give a tablespoonful at a time.

Egg and Wine, 125 Calories[5]

1 egg
½ cup cold water
Sugar
1 wineglass sherry
Nutmeg

Beat the egg. Heat the water and wine together but not boiling; pour onto the egg, stirring constantly; flavor with sugar and nutmeg.

Egg Lemonade, 192 Calories

1 egg
2 tablespoons sugar
2 tablespoons lemon juice
1 cup cold water

Beat the egg thoroughly, add the sugar and lemon juice; pour in gradually the water, stirring until smooth and well mixed. Strain and serve. Two tablespoons of sherry or port may be added if desired.

Malted Milk and Egg, 120 Calories

1 tablespoon Horlick's Malted Milk
1 tablespoon crushed fruit
1 egg
20 drops acid phosphate
1 tablespoon crushed ice
¾ cup ice water

Mix the malted milk powder, crushed fruit and egg and beat five minutes. Add the phosphate and crushed ice, blending thoroughly. Strain and add ice water or cold carbonated water, and a grating of nutmeg to flavor.

Stokes Mixture

Eggs and brandy 196 calories.

"2 egg yolks, 50 c. c. of brandy, 120 c. c. of aqua aurantii florun (sugar or syrup enough to sweeten), has considerable nutritive, as well as stimulative value, and is eligible for use when such a combination is indicated."

Grape Yolk, 150 Calories

1 egg
1 tablespoon sugar
Speck salt
2 tablespoons Welch's Grape Juice

Separate egg. Beat yolk, add sugar and stand aside while the white is thoroughly whipped. Add the grape juice to the yolk and pour this onto the whipped white, blending carefully. Serve cold. Have all ingredients chilled before blending.

Grape Juice and Egg, 270 Calories

1 egg
½ cup rich milk
1 tablespoon sugar
¼ cup Welch's Grape Juice

Beat yolk and white separately very light. To the yolk add milk, sugar and grape juice, and pour into glass. To the white add a little powdered sugar and a taste of grape juice. Serve on yolk mixture. Chill all ingredients before using.

Mulled Wine, 250-280 Calories

1 ounce stick cinnamon
A slight grating nutmeg
½ cup boiling water
1 egg
½ cup sherry, port or claret wine
2 tablespoons sugar

Put the spices into top of a double boiler with the water. Cover and cook over hot water ten minutes. Add wine to the spiced water and bring to the boiling point. Beat the egg to a stiff froth, add sugar and pour on the mulled wine, and beat well. Serve at once.

Albuminized Milk, 98 Calories

½ cup milk (sterile)
White 1 egg
Salt

Put milk and white of egg in a glass fruit jar, cover with air tight cap and rubber band. Shake until thoroughly blended. Strain into glass. A few grains of salt may be added if desired. Two teaspoons of Sanatogen added 30 calories.

NOTE.—The blending may be done in a lemonade shaker.

Albuminized Water, 13 Calories[6]

½ cup ice-cold water (boiled and chilled)
White 1 egg
Lemon juice
Sugar

Blend as for "Albuminized Milk," serve plain or add lemon juice and sugar to taste. If set on ice to keep cool, shake before serving. Two teaspoons of Sanatogen added 30 calories.

Albumin Water (for infants), 13 Calories

Albumin water is utilized chiefly in cases of acute stomach and intestinal disorders in which some nutritious and easily assimilated food is needed; albumin water is then very useful. The white of one egg is dissolved in eight ounces or a pint of water which has been boiled and cooled.

—Koplik.

Albuminized Clam Water, 18 Calories

1 cup cold water
Clam Broth
White 1 egg

To the water add the required amount of the clam broth to make the strength desired, add the unbeaten white of egg, and follow general directions for "Albuminized Milk." Serve cold in dainty glasses. This is a very nutritious drink, and will be retained by the stomach when other nourishment is rejected.

NOTE.—Milk may be substituted for the water.

Albuminized Orange, 30 Calories[7]

White 1 egg
Juice 1 orange
Sugar

To the unbeaten white add the orange juice, sweeten to taste and blend thoroughly. Strain and set on ice to cool. Serve cold.

Albuminized Sherry, 22 Calories[7]

White 1 egg
¾ tablespoon sherry
Sugar

Beat the white stiff, add slowly, while beating, the wine and sugar. Serve cold.

NOTE.—Have all ingredients cold before blending.

Albuminized Grape Juice, 40 Calories[7]

2 tablespoons Welch's Grape Juice
White 1 egg
Sugar
Chopped ice

Put in a dainty glass the grape juice, and the beaten white of egg and a little pure chopped ice; sprinkle sugar over the top and serve.

STARCHY BEVERAGES

Starchy drinks consist of cereals or cereal products, cooked thoroughly in a large amount of water and strained before serving. Arrowroot, cornstarch, tapioca, rice and rice flour are nearly pure starch. Oats, barley and wheat in forms which include the whole grains contain besides starch some protein and fat, and also valuable mineral matter, especially phosphorous, iron, and calcium salts. In starchy drinks these ingredients are necessarily present in small amounts; hence they have little energy value, unless milk or other highly nutritive material is added. Such drinks are of value when only a small quantity of nutriment can be taken.

Principles of Cooking. As the chief ingredient is starch, long cooking is necessary, in water at a high temperature (212° F.), which softens the cellulose, and breaks open the starch grains, changing the insoluble starch to soluble starch and dextrin, so that it can be readily digested.

Time of cooking should be conscientiously kept by the clock.

Digestion. The action of ptyalin is very rapid, and if these drinks are sipped slowly, so as to be thoroughly mixed with saliva, a considerable portion of starch may be changed to sugar before reaching the intestines.

Barley Water, 180 Calories

2 tablespoons pearl barley
1 quart cold water

Wash barley, add cold water and let soak several hours or over night; in same water, boil gently over direct heat two hours, or in a double boiler steadily four hours, down to one pint if used for infant feeding, and to one cup for the adult. Strain through muslin.

NOTE.—Cream or milk and salt may be added, or lemon juice and sugar. Barley water is an astringent or demulcent drink used to reduce laxative condition.

Rice Water, 100 Calories[8]

2 tablespoons rice
3 cups cold water
Salt
Milk

Wash the rice; add cold water and soak thirty minutes, heat gradually to boiling point and cook one hour or until rice is tender. Strain, reheat and dilute with boiling water or hot milk to desired consistency. Season with salt.

NOTE.—Sugar may be added if desired, and cinnamon, if allowed, may be cooked with it, and will assist in reducing a laxative condition.

Barley Water (infant feeding) 19 Calories

> 1 teaspoon barley flour
> 2 tablespoons cold water
> 1 pint boiling water

Blend flour and cold water to a smooth paste in top of double boiler; add gradually the boiling water. Boil over direct heat five minutes, stirring constantly, then put over boiling water and cook 15 minutes longer, stirring frequently. Older infants take the barley water in much more concentrated form. Barley water is used as a diluent with normal infants and in forms of diarrhœa.

NOTE.—For children or adults, use ½ tablespoon barley or rice flour, 1 cup boiling water, ¼ teaspoon salt.

Rice Water No. II, 160 Calories

> 3 tablespoons rice
> 1 pint boiling water
> 1 tablespoon stoned raisins

Wash rice, put into saucepan with water and raisins; boil gently for one hour. Strain. When cold serve. Sugar or salt may be added to taste.

NOTE.—Do not use raisins in bowel trouble.

Oatmeal Water, 50 Calories

> 1 tablespoon oatmeal
> 1 tablespoon cold water
> Speck salt
> 1 quart boiling water

Mix oatmeal and cold water, add salt and stir into the boiling water. Boil three hours; replenish the water as it boils away. Strain through a fine sieve or cheese cloth. Season, serve cold. Different brands of oatmeal vary considerably in the amount of water which they take up in cooking, and sufficient should always be added to make this drink almost as thin as water.

Oatmeal Water No. II, 220 Calories[9]

½ cup fine oatmeal
1 quart water

Use sterile water (boiled and cooled). Add oatmeal and stand in warm place (covered), for one and one-half hours. Strain, season, and cool. Sometimes used for dyspeptics.

Toast Water, 350 Calories

1 cup stale bread toasted
1 cup boiling water
Salt

Cut bread in thin slices and in inch squares. Dry thoroughly in oven until crisp and a delicate brown. Measure, and break into crumbs; add the water and let it stand one hour. Rub through a fine strainer, season and serve hot or cold. The nourishment of the bread is easily absorbed in this way and valuable in cases of fever or extreme nausea.

NOTE.—Milk or cream and sugar may be added.

Crust Coffee

Take some pieces and crusts of brown bread and dry them in a slow oven until thoroughly hard and crisp. Place in a mortar and pound or roll. Pour boiling water over and let soak for about fifteen minutes. This when strained carefully is very acceptable to invalids who are tired of the ordinary drinks, such as lemonade, etc.

Cracker Panada, 100 Calories

4 hard crackers
1 quart water
Sugar

Break crackers into pieces and bake quite brown; add water and boil fifteen minutes, allow to stand three or four minutes. Strain off the liquid through a fine wire sieve; season with salt and a little sugar. This is a nourishing beverage for infants that are teething, and with the addition of a little wine and nutmeg, is often prescribed for invalids recovering from a fever.

Bread Panada, 162 Calories

1½ cups water
1 tablespoon sugar
2 tablespoons stale white bread crumbs

¼ cup white wine
1 tablespoon lemon juice
Nutmeg

Put water and sugar on to cook, just before it commences to boil add the bread crumbs; stir well, and let it boil three or four minutes. Add the wine, lemon and a grating of nutmeg; let it boil up once more, remove from fire, and keep it closely covered until it is wanted for use.

THE COOK SAYS

Cook has discovered some little things which help to make her dishes so much above the average.

When next making griddle cakes add a little brown sugar or molasses to the batter, the cakes will brown better and more easily.

Pie crust is best kept cold in the making; to this end an excellent substitute for a rolling pin is a bottle filled with ice water.

When boiling turnips, add a little sugar to the water; it improves the flavor of the vegetables and lessens the odor in the cooking.

Hard boiled eggs should be plunged into cold water as soon as they are removed from the saucepan. This prevents a dark ring from appearing round the yolk.

Instead of mixing cocoa with boiling water to dissolve it, try mixing it with an equal amount of granulated sugar and then pouring it into the boiling water in the pot, stirring all the while.

What gave her peas she served such a nice color and taste was the adding of a lettuce leaf and a tablespoon of sugar.

Do not cover rising bread in bowls and tins with a dry cloth. Instead, cover with a damp cloth which has been wrung out of warm water. In cold weather the damp cloth should be placed over a dry cloth.

As a result, the dough will not dry on the top and the loaves when baked will be much more uniform.

To prevent holes appearing in brown bread prick twice with needle, once when the loaves are placed in tins and once immediately before loaves are placed in the oven.

Cake Hints

For those who would excel in cake making these admonitions are offered:

First—Cream the shortening.

Second—Add sugar slowly and cream it again.

Third—Add yolks of eggs well beaten.

Fourth—Mix and sift the dry ingredients.

Fifth—Add the dry materials to the mixture, which has the baking powder in it; alternate flour and liquid.

Sixth—Cut and fold in (do not beat or stir) the whites of eggs which are beaten to a dry stiff froth.

Seventh—Have a fire and pans ready. Put the cake into the oven quickly; remember that the oven can wait, but the cake never. Bake according to rule.

To test the oven heat—A hot oven will brown flour in five minutes; or you can try if you can hold the hand in it and count twenty.

Time of baking—Layer cakes, 20 or 25 minutes; loaf cakes, from 40 to 80 minutes; gem cakes, from 20 minutes to half an hour.

Never bang the oven door. The cake will fall if you do.

To prevent icing from cracking when it cuts add a teaspoon sweet cream to each unbeaten egg. When boiling syrup for icing add a pinch of cream of tartar.

Brown sugar frosting which will not crack is made of one tablespoon of vinegar, brown sugar enough to mix and the beaten white of half an egg. Beat all well together and add sugar enough to spread.

I have many times been asked how I retained the color of preserved fruits. I allow for all preserves equal measure of sugar and fruit.

It is impossible to have success if you make large quantities. I never make over three pints at a time—usually one quart.

The same method applies to all preserves. If possible, I extract some juice to start with. I then put this with one quart of sugar, (no water if the fruit contains plenty of juice, but if not, I add a little water). Allow this to boil until thick then have fruit ready to drop in; when it boils up, remove scum, and, as the juice is extracted by the boiling, dip off and allow only enough to thicken quickly.

This juice can be used for sauces, beverages of all kinds—Fruit darkens on account of continued boiling.

ECONOMICAL SOAP

Soap without boiling, will float if not too much ham or bacon drippings are used.

Into 1 quart of cold water dissolve the contents of one can of Babbits potash or lye. Melt to luke warm heat, 6 lbs, (light weight) of clean drippings that have been strained through cheesecloth several times.

Before adding the lye to the strained grease, add 1 large cupful of borax. Stir lye into kettle containing grease and stir constantly until very thick. Pour into a pan, score; in 10 or 12 hours turn out of pan and let dry. A little perfume may be added if you wish. Lamb drippings makes the finest soap.

FOOTNOTES:

[1] Calculated with 1 tablespoon brandy. 277 calories if brandy is omitted.

[2] Without liquor.

[3] Without liquor.

[4] Calculated with milk.

[5] Without sugar.

[6] Without lemon juice or sugar.

[7] Without milk.

[8] Without Milk.

[9] Estimated on one-half the oatmeal.

[10] Without sugar.